FASTLANE F₹EEDOM

"ENHANCING LIVES OF MILLIONS"

A Product of Fastlane Freedom with Vision of Enhancing Lives of Millions

---

The Wealth Code: Volume-1

"Enhancing Lives of Millions"

Vinod Singh

"Connect the Vision"
Nexus Stories Publication
Bharata

NEXUS STORIES PUBLICATION®
Surat, Gujarat, India.

Title – The Wealth Code: Volume-1

First Published by Nexus Stories Publication 2024

ISBN # 978-81-980787-5-9

Author: Vinod Singh
Contact: +91 8980026145
Email: fastlanefreedom7@gmail.com

Publication

Nexus Stories Publication®, Surat (Gujarat), Bhārata
www.nexus-stories.com # +91 87800 80718

Preface

The preface of "The Wealth Code: Volume-1" by Vinod Singh introduces the book as a key to unlocking financial freedom and creating a prosperous life. The title itself, "The Wealth Code," reflects the author's approach to building wealth systematically, much like cracking a code. Mr. Singh draws upon his personal experiences, insights, and strategies developed through years of hard work and learning. He believes that wealth isn't just about accumulating money, but about living with purpose and enhancing the quality of life for oneself and others.

Mr. Singh positions the book as more than just a financial guide; it is a product of Fastlane Freedom, a movement aimed at empowering individuals to achieve financial independence while contributing positively to the world. He emphasizes that this volume is not a quick-fix solution but a long-term vision to enhance the lives of millions, encouraging readers to adopt a mindset of growth, responsibility, and service.

The preface highlights how Singh's journey to financial freedom was driven by his desire to help others escape the limitations of traditional monetary systems. Through "The Wealth Code", readers are invited to learn principles that transcend conventional approaches to wealth, focusing on sustainable methods that benefit individuals and their communities.

In summary, the preface sets the tone for a comprehensive guide that blends practical wealth-building strategies with a broader vision of financial freedom, aimed at uplifting society while achieving personal success.

- KB Joshi (Director, Nexus Stories Publication)

Profile

About Us

Fastlane Freedom was launched in 2019 by Vinod Singh, a Belief Changer, following 3.5 years of research on mindfulness and its relationship to money. Fastlane Freedom is motivated by a vision of **'Enhancing Millions'** by transforming people's mindsets to improve their financial conditions. Vinod has 16 years of professional experience and is dedicated to offering high-quality, practical content on Mindfulness, Money, Business, Parenting, and Student Life.

Countless people throughout the world suffer as a result of incorrect ideas that add stress to their financial, personal, professional, commercial, and social life. To address this, we provide insights based on scientific data, real-life case studies, and our own knowledge.

Profile of Mr. Vinod Singh

Essentially, he comes from a farming background. After finishing his engineering degree (B. Tech, Mechanical), he has started his career and worked from well-known MNCs.

He has been studying "How Beliefs Affect Our Life, Especially Financial Life" for almost 7 years. The study began with the question, "Why are some people financially successful for generations while others are not?"

He launched his blogging website, www.fastlanefreedom.com, in January 2021. This website contains informative and life-changing posts (now over 1000) on themes such as mindfulness, money, business growth, parenting, student life, and popular quotes.

As a serial entrepreneur, till now he has covered thousands of Peoples /Students /Businessmen / Professions and also connected with several MSME & Corporate groups.

Scan the QR code to connect with his profile.

*****

Index

1. Self-Limiting Beliefs about Money – Keeping You Away From It!

What is a self-limiting belief? Any belief that is not helping you to grow in life, we can call it a self-limiting belief. These beliefs might be affecting your personal life, financial life, and family life and the more interesting is you might not be aware of it.

Belief Scams in our Life!

When it comes to money, we are surrounded by so many not-so-financially capable people. We are scripted by friends, parents, teachers, government, schools, banks, corporate, etc. for thinking in a decided manner. *How our parents /close relatives set perceptions in our minds about money, has a long-lasting impact on us.*

What is your financial limit? Why limit, can you double or triple it? Have you ever dreamed of being rich beyond your current limit, which is really in your mind?

A small child asks so many questions and has so many dreams, but slowly when they grow and start going to school things start changing. When they passed out 10th /12th they generally stop asking such questions and have very limited dreams. Something peculiar thing happens in school with the support of teachers, friends, parents, media, news, government, etc.

"If you accept a limiting belief, then it will become a truth for you"-Louise L.
We stop living our lives openly and seek Security at each and every stage in life. That is true for our financial life aspect also.

I came across in ***book titled UnScripted by MJ DeMarco***; The Belief Scams (Lies we believe). How these belief scams affect various aspects of our life and held true like the ancient proverb **"three men make a tiger".**

Belief#1: *the shortcut scam; "ordinary doesn't compel extraordinary"* (99 % of people believe in events and only 1 % in process).

Belief#2: *the special scam; "I am not good at that" (99 % operate with fixed mindset and only 1 % with growth mindset)*

Belief#3: *the consumption scam; how much time did that cost? (99 % want to be the consumer side only 1 % want to be producer)*

Belief#4: *the money scam; I can get rich by wanting to get rich. (99 % wish to be rich, only 1 % believe in value addition)*

Belief#5: *the poverty scam: I am poor because you are rich (99% operate with selfish mode, only 1 % operate with selfless mode)*

Belief#6: *luck scam: you don't play, you don't win (99% believe in luck, 1% believe in probability)*

Belief#7: *the frugality scam: Live poor, die rich (99% want to be defence, only 1% want to be offence)*

Belief#8: *the compound interest scam: Wall Street ain't make ya rich (99% believe power of compound interest in creating wealth, 1 % believe in creating additional income sources)*

Way to come out from these self-limiting beliefs:

Challenge in Change Management

Reward of Change Management!

Once you are aware of the self-limiting beliefs about money, the next step is to come out of it. There are several ways to come out of such false beliefs.

Start observing your environment, like people say that money doesn't grow on tree! Look closely that there are so many plants available all around us.

People are owning rental properties, which in turn give money to the owner continuously. Can we not call it a money tree? Some other people have done business set-up, which is run by their team and now they are earning a good amount of money from this. Don't you think that this is working as a money tree!

Our society is full of such examples and has tons of money trees.

The problem is not in money, but the meaning we associate with money. The love of money, not money, is the root of all kinds of evil. So change your self-limiting beliefs about money.

We need to take control of something, which seems uncontrollable; our environment. If we live in an environment that is full of broke people, a high level of chance is for us to remain broke.

Fame or physical talent is not a prerequisite to wealth. Almost every day REAL success stories about normal human beings are getting published in newspapers and magazines. You can find several such examples around yourself, in your society, in your friend circle, in your relatives, etc. These persons were below normal or normal at one point in time but now they are very successful financially. Just have a close watch on them, they have changed their thought process, and their self-limiting belief to come out from their not-so-good condition.

Financial discipline is blind to income!! Whether you are earning 2 million or 20K. We many a time increase our earnings but at the same time our expenditure also increases, so end result is our life remain in struggle. We are just a few months away from being broke i.e. we need to borrow either from a friend or relative or a bank to survive.

The attraction of positive /negative thoughts: on which to focus? The one who lives in your mind expands. If all the time we thought about our financial problems, they will keep coming. So the right strategy is to shift our focus from scarcity to abundance. If our thought is filled with abundance then surely things are going to change in the coming time.

Admire rich/wealthy people, if you want to be! If we see each rich person as a Bad Guy, then we may remain broke for a long time as we are feeding contradictory thoughts to our subconscious mind, which controls 90 % of our life. One thought is that you want to be rich and another thought is that you are not happy seeing other rich people. Here mind confuses and leads you nowhere, you remain in the same financial condition for a long time even some time for a complete life. Many a time people wonder about what they did their whole time for themselves and for their children. They leave their children at the same juncture where they had started even after one complete generation gap.

Money makes you more what you already are (greed/strong/help etc.). Money does not make you bad unless you are already! So better if you change your self-limiting beliefs.

Without a target of money amount & end dates nothing moves. So I would say, have a positive thought process about money if you want to improve your financial life and do your Karma to attain your financial goal. Once things sink into your subconscious mind then miracles happen!

*****

2. How Debt Take Control of Our Life? Understand the basic reasons behind!

A person's life revolves around debt. There are several examples where we see individual or company is growing at a good pace, earning is growing so does the spending. Many a time net result is NIL or Negative. Debt can be good if you are investing that money for a higher return than borrowed one but if you are taking it for day-to-day needs/luxuries then it's not good at all. If second is the case then there are good chances that you are in a debt trap like one EMI is getting over, another starts.

Reasons for Debt/Debt Cycle/Bad Finance

- If Buying Insurance policies for investment purpose (95 out of 100 people buy like that only). For insurance purpose, term plan can be the better choice.
- Use of Credit Card and then missing payment due date (Extreme high-interest rate applied if you didn't pay the full amount on Due date. Even minimum payment option doesn't work well)
- We are not having any idea of the power of compounding on our investment & we avoid investment in our early life. *Albert Einstein said that the power of compounding is the eighth wonder of the world.*

- Buying stocks based on tips without any knowledge and then losing money.
- Buying things just because they are on discount & the funny thing is now you will find such discounted sales every other month
- Getting tempted to go for a foreign trip just because some of your friend/relative/colleagues put a post on Facebook and Instagram
- Spending a bomb on weekend parties (5 days' work & 2 days' party: This is a new culture)
- No track of cash flow (time & again every month end same situation)
- No emergency budget (No Udhari Fund)
- Spending all the hard-earned money on children marriage
- No medical insurance, a hefty amount gone if one medical emergency comes up in the family.
- No financial plan, People do not know why they need to save money because they don't know their financial goals.
- Buying excessive gold only to keep it in the locker and many a time putting this gold to take a loan and paying interest on that borrowed amount.
- An extremely conservative approach with investment, all the negative news/updates will be checked for that investment and finally, investment ideas go for a toss! Procrastinating investment decisions (from tomorrow).
- Lack of clarity between asset and liability (e.g. Car can be an asset if you are buying it for Cash or on

very minimum finance, but buying a car on maximum finance then this is going to be a liability.

- A lot of people confuse economic spending with being cheap.
- Spending a lot of money on fancy stuff / Gadgets.
- Lack of patience to return from investment, each of wants to see the quick return.
- Depending upon others for investment decisions (Lack of self-knowledge on the subject)
- Not discussing the money matters in the family, keeping children away. This type of decision brings a similar situation in front of each generation as there is no learning transferred to the next generation.
- People blindly invest their money in penny stocks, day trading, futures, and options.
- Wasting time on unproductive things & no time to increase their knowledge on investment skills.
- Instead of spending what is *left after investing*, people invest what is *left after spending.*
- Root Cause: Lack of knowledge about personal financial management!!
- Personal finance is 80 percent behavior and only 20 percent head knowledge.
- Most of us know what to do; we just have trouble doing it. How do you lose weight? By regular work-out and keeping diet discipline. But in spite of knowing this fact how many follow this discipline!
- The Great Depression permanently changed the way many people handled their money.

- In our case, that would be borrowing lots of money and not saving any because "my job is stable. I can afford the 'easy payments' with my job."
- The enemy of "the best" is not "the worst." The enemy of "the best" is "just fine." Almost similar pattern we follow on our investments.
- It is human nature to want it and want it now; it is also a sign of immaturity. Being willing to delay pleasure for a greater result is a sign of maturity.
- The Red-Faced Kid ("I want it, and I want it now!") rules your life, you will stay broke!
- We buy things we don't need with money we don't have in order to impress people we don't like.
- We don't ask "How much?" to pay with cash/Debit card and instead ask, "How much down, and how much a month?"
- The vast majority of college seniors have credit card debt before they even have a job!

<u>Way Head Thoughts!</u>

- *<u>Larry Burkett</u> said debt is not the problem; it is the symptom.*
- The borrower truly is a slave to the lender.
- Your income is your greatest wealth-building tool, not debt.
- Most people concentrate on the urgent in our culture. We worry about our health and focus on our money only after they're gone.
- "A budget is people telling their money where to go instead of wondering where it went."

- No one is born with the knowledge of how to handle money.
- With Money, ignorance doesn't mean foolish; it means you have to learn how to manage it.
- "What you don't know won't hurt you" is a really a foolish statement. What you don't know about money will make you broke and keep you broke.
- Remember, if you want to be thin and muscular, you should study the habits of people who are thin and muscular. If you want to be rich, you should study the habits and value systems of the rich.
- We've car payments and credit-card payments—there's never been a time when we were debt-free. We avoid discussing money because it would always end with an argument or someone's feelings getting hurt.
- Continuing to do the same thing over and over again and expecting a different result is the definition of insanity.
- Money won't behave unless you tame it.
- "Money is an excellent slave and a horrible master."
- Brian Tracy, the motivational speaker, says, "What does it take to succeed on a big scale? A tremendous God-given talent? Inherited wealth? A decade of postgraduate education? Connections? Fortunately for most of us, what it takes is something very simple and accessible: clear, written goals." According to Brian Tracy, a study of Harvard graduates found that after two years, the 3 percent who had written goals achieved more financially than the other 97 percent combined!

- We have learned that getting a hold of your attitude is the number one factor in being victorious over your finances.
- Student loans are cancer. Once you have them, you can't get rid of them. They are like an unwelcome relative who comes to stay for a "few days" and is still in the guest room ten years later.
- It's unbelievable the feeling of freedom that comes when you don't have the weight of payments hanging over your head.
- The bottom line is that it is easy to become wealthy if you don't have any payments.
- If you really believe that wealth building will no longer be a dream but a reality if you have no payments, you should be willing to do bizarre and sacrificial things to have no payments. Time to pay off the DEBT!
- The sexes do view the emergency budget (*No Udhari_Fund*) differently. In general, men are more task-oriented, and ladies are more security-based.
- When your money makes more than you do, you are officially wealthy. When you can comfortably live on your investment income, you are financially secure. Money is a hard worker, harder than you. It never gets sick, never gets pregnant, and is never disabled. Money works twenty-four hours a day, seven days a week.
- Only the strong can help the weak, and that is true of money too. A toddler is not allowed to carry a newborn; only adults who have the muscular strength to ensure safety should carry babies. If you want to help someone, many times you can't do so without money.

Short Story:

"Eric Butterworth tells of an interesting system used to capture monkeys in the jungle. The captors use heavy glass bottles with long necks. Into each bottle they deposit some sweet-smelling nuts. The aroma of the nuts attracts a monkey to the bottle.

When the monkey puts its hand into the bottle to get the nuts, the neck of the bottle is too small for its fist to come back out. The monkey can't take his hand out of the bottle without dropping the nuts, which he is unwilling to do.

The bottles are too heavy to carry away, so the monkey becomes trapped by nothing more than greed. We may smile at these foolish monkeys, but how many times has our freedom been taken away by nothing more than our greed?"

*****

3. How Debt Trap Begin? Break the EMI pattern

Debt trap! Is it not a fearful word? We live a financial life in which we are just a few weeks or a few months away from being broke. There are several examples like If we didn't get the next business deal, if we lose our job, if we miss the next endorsement contract as a celebrity we are going to be broke.

We focus on earning but in parallel, our expenditures also increase. When our expenditure is more than the income, what is the outcome; to borrow from someone to fill the gap e.g. if your monthly income is Rs. 30,000 and expenditure for the month is Rs. 35,000, then you need to borrow the differential amount of Rs. 5,000 to manage the things.

We manage this situation for few months, then this pattern becomes a part of our subconscious mind i.e. mind registers one pattern of financial deficit and all the emotion associated with it. As the subconscious mind is neutral, it doesn't understand positive emotion or negative emotion. Anyway when we are in debt, can we have positive emotions, hardly; most of the time we have negative emotions.

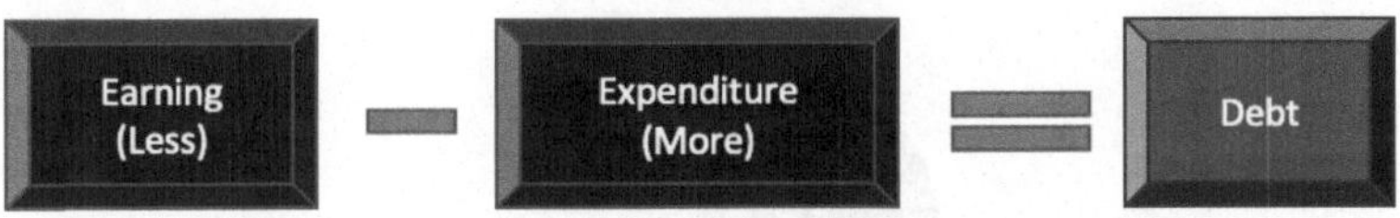

Now, this is something interesting, suppose in one particular month your earning is more than your expenditure and you are having surplus money. In this situation, your subconscious mind will suggest you something like buying additional stuff, or some mean to spend your surplus or even more than surplus.

Why does it do so? Because it wants to give you the same feeling which you are experiencing every month. It's true, how many times we fall into the trap of credit card buying. We buy something using a credit card, why are we using a credit card, to earn points or we are not having money in our account but we want that particular thing immediately.

We get extra time to pay on credit card purchases. If the amount is more then we prefer to convert that amount in EMI or at the time of purchase only we ask the seller to convert our credit card purchase into EMI.

If you do this once or twice, there is a good chance that when you are near to your last payment of EMI, some other thing will pop-up to purchase in a similar pattern and other EMI will start e.g. we buy big-screen TV from discounted sell on the credit card.

EMI Trap Continue!

Now in the last two EMI payments, there might be a demand for a new fridge or mobile or holiday package which is also with additional advantage if we buy through credit card.

As we are not able to pay the full amount on the due date (in the world more than 70 % of people don't pay credit card payment on the due date), then we ask to convert that purchase to EMI. So EMI trap continues.

Here no means, I am saying that we should not buy things on a credit card, what I am saying that we should not fall into the trap on EMIs as it hardly ends.

We become habitual of this trap and many a time pay hefty interest charges in-between while conversion of purchase in EMI or not paying the full amount on the due date.

Debt & Your Life Time!

People do not realize that they spend more than 50% of their lifetime to pay the debt. If you bought Rs. 30,000 TV by borrowing money and if your net income is also Rs.30000, then logically you have booked 26 days (Working day in the month) x 08 hours (Working hours per day)=208 hours of your life for this TV payment.

Again, I no mean saying that you should not buy a TV, what I am saying is that buy when you have money with cash or debit card. We must give focus on our earning and constantly improve the means. But we become Red-Faced child, who need the toy (things) right now, so we do better deals but with a credit card and become happy with earned points on that purchase.

We are so much used to listen to peoples around us and also from Banks that we cannot even imagine buying Rs 30,000 component with Cash. When we buy items in cash, we can ask for a good discount.

Time and again one thing is coming out that we get a reflection of what we keep in our mind most of the time. If all the time dept is there, we shall get the situations to support this thought as this is controlled by your beliefs and your subconscious mind.

Own Painful Experience of Debt

I have personally gone through this pain for more than one year. Short of some amount almost every month then I borrowed money from my friend or relatives. Then I changed this cycle after applying principles from one book on the subject. As I was only one month away from debt-free life, so I changed my thought process. I had managed for one month, then for the complete year and till now.

One thing I realize during my transition is that most people are not having financial knowledge and really don't want to discuss those financial matters with anyone. So from where wisdom comes to rescue us unless otherwise, we have financially smart friends/relatives from whom we can learn or read good literature on this subject. If we train our mind to take good care while dealing with finance, it does. Whatever we focus on, It expands, so does it happens in our financial condition also.

Way ahead Discipline (Investment)!

Many a time earning amount is not important, more important is discipline to spend the money in a more logical way, <u>investing it regularly</u>. Preferring investing over spending i.e. when we receive or salary, payment investment should have priority overspending. Once we set an investment pattern, our mind supports our every movement. Remember, at this time don't keep fear of losing in mind all the time, if this thought sink in your subconscious mind, there is a good chance that you will lose your money. So always have wealth/money abundance thoughts.

Thought:

"A scarcity mindset can cause you to limit yourself through your beliefs and actions, preventing you from achieving your biggest goals, keeping you in debt, or destroying your confidence."- Anonymous

*****

4. Your Financial Thermostat! - Internal & External Laws of Money

We are having a desire to improve our financial condition but in reality, we are not able to change it. Why? There is a missing link between our desire for success and our achievement of success. These are two different worlds altogether i.e. having desire and actual achievement.

No doubt you've read other blogs, watched YouTube videos, gone to courses, attended seminars, and learned about numerous get-rich systems be they in real estate, stocks, or business. But what happened? For most people, not much! They get a short blast of energy, and then it's back to the status quo. Finally, there's an answer. It's simple, it's law, and you're not going to remember it.

It all comes down to this: if your subconscious "financial blueprint" is not "set" for success, nothing you learn, nothing you know, and nothing you do will make much of a difference. "It's not an exact science, but for the most part, rich people think a certain way and poor people think a completely different way, and those ways of thinking determine their actions and therefore determine their results."

Internal & External Laws of Money

There are "external" & "internal" laws of money. The external laws include things like business knowledge, money management, and investment plans etc. These are essential. But the internal laws are important. An analogy would be a sculpture and his tools. Having top-of-the-line tools is imperative, but being the top-notch sculpture who masterfully uses those tools is even more critical.

"It's not enough to be in the right place at the right time. You have to be the right person in the right place at the right time."- T. Harv Eker

So who are we? How do we think? What are our beliefs? What are our habits and traits? How do we really feel about ourself? Are we having confidence in in ourself? How well we manage in difficult situation? How much do we trust others? ***Do we truly feel that we deserve wealth/money?***

What is our ability to act in spite of fear, in spite of worry, in spite of inconvenience, in spite of discomfort? Can we act when we're not in the mood? ***The fact is that our character, our thinking, and our beliefs are a critical part of what determines the level of our financial success.***

"Capital as such is not evil; it is its wrong use that is evil. Capital in some form or other will always be needed."- **Gandhiji**

When our inner world is not capable enough to manage money; whether small or large, outer world (realty) will also reflect in same way. We see TV shows, Lottery winners who get very high amount of money, for how long they maintain that money? They lose that money in maximum five years and reach in same position which was there earlier. Now you know the real cause.

On the outside it looks like bad luck, a downturn in the economy, a lousy partner, whatever. On the inside, however, it's another matter. That's why, if we come into big money when we're not ready for it on the inside, the chances are our wealth will be short-lived and we will lose it. The vast majority of people simply do not have the internal capacity to create and hold on to large amounts of money.

Managing & Increasing money after earning is almost ten time harder. Lot of difficulties increases with increase amount on money, we had to train ourself to manage all these difficulties well. These show winners /Lottery winners were not ready and their thermostat was set for less amount, they spend all the surplus money in different means and come to original state at which their thermostat was set. Trust me, our subconscious mind a vital role here as well.

On the other hand, the opposite occurs for self-made millionaires. Notice that when self-made millionaires lose their money, they usually have it back within a relatively short time.

Why does this phenomenon occur? Because even though some self-made millionaires may lose their money, they never lose the most important ingredient to their success: their millionaire mind. Most people's financial thermostats are set for generating thousands, not millions of dollars; some people's financial thermostats are set for generating hundreds, not even thousands; and some people's financial thermostats are set for below zero.

Research shows that 80 percent of individuals will never be financially free in the way they'd like to be, and 80 percent will never claim to be truly happy.

<u>You Reap What You Sow!</u>

Imagine a tree. Let's suppose this tree represents the tree of life. On this tree there are fruits. In life, our fruits are called our results. So we look at the fruits (our results) and we don't like them; there aren't enough of them, they're too small, or they don't taste good. So what do we tend to do?

Most of us put even more attention and focus on the fruits, our results. But what is it that actually creates those particular fruits? It's the seeds and the roots that create those fruits. This is what's under the ground that creates what's above the ground. It's what's invisible that creates what's visible.

So what does that mean? It means that if you want to change the fruits, you will first have to change the roots. ***If you want to change the visible, you must first change the invisible.***

For example, let's suppose you've just written a letter on your computer. You hit the print key and the letter comes out of your printer. You look at your hard copy, and lo and behold, you find a typo. So you take out your trusty eraser and rub out the typo. Then you hit print again and outcomes the same typo. Oh my gosh, how could this be? You just erased it! So this time you get a bigger eraser and you rub even harder and longer.

You even study a three-hundred-page manual called Effective Erasing. Now you've got all the "tools" and knowledge you need. You're ready. You hit print and there it is again! "No way!" you cry out, stunned in amazement. "How could this be? What's going on here? Am I in the twilight zone?" What's going on here is that the real problem cannot be changed in the "printout," the physical world; it can only be changed in the "program," the mental, emotional, and spiritual worlds.

What you cannot see in this world is far more powerful than anything you can see. You may or may not agree with this statement, but to the extent that you do not apply this principle in your life, you must be suffering. Why? Because you are going against the laws of nature, whereby what is under the ground creates what is above the ground, where what is invisible creates what is visible.

A lack of money is never, ever a problem. A lack of money is merely a symptom of what is going on underneath. Lack of money is the effect, but what is the root cause? It boils down to this. The only way to change your "outer" world is to first change your "inner" world.

Whatever results you're getting, be they rich or poor, good or bad, positive or negative, always remember that your outer world is simply a reflection of your inner world. If things aren't going well in your outer life, it's because things aren't going well in your inner life. It's that simple.

I am really thankful to T. Harv Eker for Writing many of the above scientific principles on finance in the Book "The Secrets of Millionaire Mind: Mastering the Inner Game of Wealth". Till now I have applied so many principles in my own life to change my Thermostat of financial amount.

*****

5. No Udhari (Borrow) Fund! – How to build and maintain it?

No Udhari Fund helps you in day-to-day life to avoid borrowing money from friends, relatives, colleagues, banks. It may require paying EMI, purchase of a household item, Medical emergency in the family, Vehicle repair work, Shopping for function at home, etc. We borrow this money because we are just managing our routine monthly expenditure from our income and this is something additional, for which we were not ready. Many a time this amount is less but we have no other choice but to borrow as we cannot ignore these items. We generally manage to pay back this borrowed money in the next couple of months.

But actually, what happens after some time, when you are on the verge of paying your borrowed money, some other thing pop-up, for which you need to borrow again. When this happens, your life sucks. You feel so low on energy and think, what is happening in your life? Why things are not in your control?

<u>One EMI After Another EMI</u>

I share one real story of one of my contact, he was a bachelor and working in a private company. As he was involved in fieldwork, so he decided to have a bike. He purchased a bike on finance. After some time, he lost his job and was not able to pay the bike's EMIs & sold that. Later he got another job and life was smooth again. After a few years, he was preparing for marriage. As he was not having money back-up so he took a personal loan from the bank to bear marriage expenditure. After marriage, he settles with his wife in the city, where he was working, managing to repay his personal loan on EMIs. After some time, he decided to take a bike, it was the same time when he was about to pay his last EMI of personal loan. He purchased the bike again on EMIs, when I meet him last time, his wife asks him for a refrigerator, it's again at the same time when he was on the verge of paying his last EMI of bike loan!

Actually, EMIs give us the power to have things before even we really become capable! Is it true? No, it actually makes us weak financially, we cannot invest our money because we are not left with any spare amount after paying these EMIs. Then the question arises, should we not fulfill our basic need even by borrowing money i.e. what is the harm to buy a bike or a refrigerator on EMIs in day-to-day life? I leave it to you now, which life you prefer; one with constant pressure to pay the EMIs / Debt or Another one having no such pressure but a life with financial abundance.

How to come out of this Debt/EMI trap in life? Is it really possible to run life without borrowing? The good news is it is very well possible if you follow certain discipline. The solution for this problem is "No Udhari Fund".

What is "No Udhari Fund (NUF) & How to Create it?

No Udhari Fund is basically one liquid money reserve, which you can use in any of the above situations without borrowing from others. For this, we need to keep aside some money from our earnings, such that the net sum is sufficient enough to run your 3-6 month period. This calls for a high level of discipline. Initially, you can plan for 3 months. Work out how much money you require if you didn't receive any money for 3 months, then start keeping aside a specific amount every month for this purpose. This cycle may take 6 to 12 months, but believe me, after these 6 or 12 months your life will be much easy.

Now let's understand further discipline on this fund, e.g. You have decided Rs. 100K as your No Udhari Fund, and suddenly any of the above situations arise like medical emergency in family costing you Rs. 30K. You have decided to use your NUF & now the net balance amount is Rs. 70K. Here comes the secret, now it's your responsibility to refill it back to Rs. 100K. If you missed this discipline, there will not be any amount balance in this fund. If there is no amount, means you have to borrow again.

People struggle to create this fund, but it is quite easy if you start step by step. Once you decide your amount & when you receive money, put X amount (maybe 5 or 10%) aside and forget that. If some more surplus is there, add that to this fund. Keep on adding until you achieve your target.

This fund, should not be at an easily accessible location. There must be some restriction to use this fund otherwise it will act as surplus money available for expenditure. You can set some rules with one of your family members like when both of you agree then only this fund will be used and once it's used, it will be refilled again in a stipulated time frame.

This fund works at all levels, only the amount varies depending on people's class of living. People generally keep a minimum of 3 months back-up, a maximum of 6 months to 12 months back. You can share this practice with your children. They can start by keeping aside some amount regularly in their piggy bank *(Gullak)*. After some time you will realize that it is all about habit as personal finance is 80 percent behavior and only 20 percent head knowledge. If you establish the habit of not borrowing money and pass that on to your children, then your life & your children's will be much easy with respect to finance.

"If you aim at nothing, you will hit it every time." - **Zig Ziglar**

So aim for debt free life not only for yourself but for your next generations by guiding them.

Brian Tracy, the motivational speaker, says, "What does it take to succeed on a big scale? A tremendous God-given talent? Inherited wealth? A decade of postgraduate education? Connections? Fortunately for most of us, what it takes is something very simple and accessible: clear, written goals." According to Brian Tracy, a study of Harvard graduates found that after two years, the 3 percent who had written goals achieved more financially than the other 97 percent combined!

*****

6. Your Investment Account! - A key to achieve financial freedom in life

Investment account plays a very important role towards financial freedom in our life. Financial freedom is the status of having enough income to pay one's living expenses for the rest of one's life without having to be employed or dependent on others. We all ***WANT*** it but how many of us really ***COMMIT*** to achieve financial freedom. Now there is a vast difference between wanting something and showing commitment to something. Want is a wish, it may get fulfilled or may not get fulfilled. If doesn't get fulfilled it will not bother you much. Want definition is "have a desire to possess or do (something); wish for." And for Commit it goes like "pledge or bind (a person or an organization) to a certain course or policy."

Investment Commitment

Once you commit to something, all the trillion of body cells and all the neurons act to support you to achieve your goal. All this happens through power of subconscious mind. This is one of the main differentiating factor, which separate success and failure. People who are successful in any field, are not wishing but always committing to achieve their desired goals.

Now once you committed to your financial freedom, one important stepping stone in this journey is to have Investment Account. An investment account is basically an account in which we keep 10 % to 50 % of our net income only for investment purposes. When you are at a very early age, you can put maximum money in this account like when you are a earning bachelor, you can reduce the percentage when your other expenses increase. There is one statistic that goes like if your yearly income is Rs. 5 Lac, then to have Rs. 5

Lac in your pocket, you need to work for 10 years. It's multiple of 10 in all the professions unless you start investing your money as early stage as possible.

I am not suggesting any particular investment plan here, what I am suggesting is to keep a minimum 10 % of your net income aside only for investment. Remember, once you are focused on investment, you will surely do better for getting a good return on investment. If you are not having good knowledge on investment, gain that, learn that but for God sake do not 100 % depend on other for your investment.

Power of regular Investment

Let's take one example, assuming your net earnings is Rs. 35K per month i.e. yearly it is Rs. 4.2 Lacs. and accordingly below are the different case scenarios with respect to your investment amount and also return on that investment.

Net Yearly Income	If 10 % in Invertment	If 20 % in Invertment	If 50 % in Invertment
4,20,000	42,000	84,000	2,10,000
% Return	Total Annual Amount (1st year)		
6%	2,520	5,040	12,600
12%	5,040	10,080	25,200
18%	7,560	15,120	37,800
% Return	Total Annual Amount (2nd year)		
6%	5,191	10,382	25,956
12%	10,685	21,370	53,424
18%	16,481	32,962	82,404
% Return	Total Annual Amount (5th year)		
6%	13,233	26,466	66,166
12%	27,855	55,711	1,39,277
18%	44,074	88,148	2,20,371
% Return	Total Annual Amount (10th year)		
6%	26,637	53,275	1,33,187
12%	56,483	1,12,983	2,82,459
18%	90,127	1,80,343	4,50,857
Amount in Rs.			

I have not considered an increment in your income and also at the same time not considered an inflation factor, i.e. if your earning is constant then also in 10th year your income from the investment is substantial. Even it's surpassing your net income of Rs 4.2 Lacs if you get an 18% return and continue to invest 50% of your net income (i.e. Rs 2.1 Lac) every year.

Now some of you might be thinking that an 18 % return is really very difficult, but I assure you that there are several investment programs such as real estate, in which there is a good chance that you can get even more than an 18 % return.

Create a Parallel you!

What will you feel by creating a parallel you (your investment money, which is earning for you)? Don't you feel excited, your money is earning money 24 X 7, without taking any type of leave, even working while you are sleeping. Are you not feeling empowered when thinking that now you are not the only earning member in your family, a parallel you is also earning? When your intensity of investment is high and there are multiple sources of income, your wealth increases in a multifold way; even you can reduce this 10-year tenure to less. <u>Think big & feel the abundance.</u>

"Money is a terrible master but an excellent servant."
- *<u>PT Barnum</u>*

*****

7. How Subconscious Learnings Impacts Our Financial Life!

Most of our beliefs and thoughts were formed during the period starting at 4.5 months in the womb to 7 years after birth when most of the learnings were subconscious. A child learns maximum till the age of 7 years by observing the environment, parents, siblings, friends, teachers, etc. This is the period in their consciousness has not started developing but the subconscious is working at its peak.

All the thoughts, and beliefs stored till this age impact life of these children lifelong. Many of these beliefs which children understood as true, may not be true.

Learning from Parents

Young children carefully observe their environment and download the worldly wisdom offered by parents directly into their subconscious memory. ***As a result, their parents' behavior and beliefs become their own.*** Most of the time, parents are also not aware of the fact that each and everything, which they are doing, will impact the lives of their children.

Struggle!

If a child has seen her parents struggle throughout this early stage, then struggle becomes part of her life also. Even when they become adults & start earning good, their subconscious mind will provide situations where they will feel the struggle. If things are going well at business or at the workplace, then the struggle may start with family relationships or with friends. One or another aspect of life will most of the time have this struggle feels. This is how our subconscious mind works. It keeps on creating the situation, which you always have in your mind. What you have in your mind is a struggle!

Problem-Solving!

If children learn from their parents to solve problems, they become the master of solving problems. Now we all know the world is full of several types of problems, and only a few peoples are there who are in the business of solving the problem. As a result, you can create a great fortune! There are several successful people, who have learned this skill at a very early stage in life and used that skill to create businesses like Bill Gates (an American business magnate), and Dhirubhai Ambani (an Indian business tycoon).

One more important thing happens, when we have caring and visionary parents, the parents who were not having opportunities, but want their children to do the things which children want. The point is, those intentions must be clear at the early stage of childhood. Like if we see Sachin Tendulkar (an Indian cricketer), we also remember his childhood image with a cricket bat.

Financial Dimensions

Middle/ Lower class kids see their parents in scarcity of money. For each small or big thing, money does not come easily. Whenever they ask their parents for a toy or a cycle or pizza, the answer is *'Beta Abhi Nahi, Abhi Paise Kam Hain'* **(Kid, not this time, we are short of money)** or parents suppress that demand completely. When such words come from parents, this kid understands that money is not an easy thing. Or some other words come as *'Paise Ped Par Nahi Ugte'* **(Money doesn't grow on the tree).**

Who said this, it is really ridiculous! Money grows on the tree, but that tree you need to plant. That tree can be any business system, rental property, or anything, which brings you money. If nothing is left to say, then this is the last taunt *'Paisa Hi Sabhi Pareshani Ke Jadh Hai'* **(Money is the root of all the problems).** Now, this dialogue is like the last nail in the coffin, as this kid will never earn a good amount of money because he has a belief that if he earns a good amount of money, he will also have problems associated with this money.

If we can not fulfill, our children's wishes, it's ok as there must be some genuine reason for that. But for God's sake don't give negative thoughts / disempowering thoughts about money because these thoughts will create issues for that child lifelong. Believe me, many people have not understood in their lifetime, why they were not successful financially in spite of earning good, why most of the time they were having issues.

Rich Environment Effects

Now, **what do rich kids learn from their parents?** They have learned systems of making money by seeing their parents or other family members. For them, money was never a problem, it was flowing freely in the family. And you might have noticed that rich kids, may not be good at studying or sports but there is a high level of chance that they are good at making money or minting money. Middle / lower class think that they (rich kids) are enjoying life on their parent's money, but many a time reality is different. They are making a good amount of money for themselves as they have learned that skill unconsciously at an early age. And this unconsciousness helps them to attain their financial goals. Once you are financially capable, you can solve not all but most of the problems with money.

The same logic of the subconscious mind applies here, whatever they had seen in childhood is controlling their life. They have understood the business concepts as a system, if that system is in place, money will pour in. So even if they are not good at academics, but they are good at developing business systems, which generates money. By this time, you might have recalled some of the rich kids, which were there in your class. Some of them were not good at exams, but now doing may be better than you financially.

Message to Parents

So, dear parents don't feel guilty for understanding this logic of the subconscious mind so late, now you have understood this. From now onwards you can guide your children or grandchildren to change their money-limiting beliefs and replace those beliefs with financial abundance beliefs. *Whatever you keep in your mind, become reality one day. So, fill your mind with peace, harmony, faith, joy, honesty, integrity, abundance, loving, kindness, and gentleness; then you will be sowing treasures in the heavens of your own mind.*

"God is the source of my supply. His riches flow to me freely, copiously, and abundantly. All my financial and other needs are met at every moment of time and point of space; there is always a divine surplus." – <u>*Joseph Murphy*</u>

*****

8. Contradictory Thoughts about Money, Keep You Away from It...

Keeping contradictory thoughts in mind about money is not at all beneficial to you. If you really want to improve your financial life. You will understand the whole logic through a short story.

How do you feel, when someday you see one of your old classmates at the city corner in his luxury-branded car. And you recall this is the same guy, to whom money was always a struggle. He was not able to buy clothes, to timely pay his fees. He hardly attended any party and could not get the job in his final year from campus, but you were the lucky ones.

Your classmate said *Hello* to you, and you also greeted him well. He talked to you for few minutes, as he was going for some important work, so he has asked for your contact number & said that he will call you later.

After this incident, what will be your feeling? Will you feel happy about your classmate? Or feel like 3 Idiots movie characters Raju & Farhan. When Rancho topped in the exam, they say as ***'we feel sad when our friend fails the exam, but we feel sadder when our friend top the exam!'***

In life, you were always wanted to have a very good financial position in society, but you are not getting success. Now suddenly you see your friend in a very rich lifestyle, you feel a little awkward. A lot of thoughts are running in your mind. How this has happened to him, you feel that he might have borrowed somebody else's car, he might be in the same situation he was there in his college days or he might be somewhere lower than my financial status.

<u>Invitation to luxury</u>

Suddenly on next day, when you were at the workplace, your phone ring. As it was an unknown number, so you picked up the call and you were surprised it was he! He said sorry for not spending time with you on that day, then asked you to visit him at his home. You said ok and decided to meet him at weekend.

When you went there, you see a royal house with all the amenities inside and also three luxury cars in his private parking. You were, once upon a time, was not believing that he was owing that car and you are again in the same situation. You thought that he might have accumulated all his wealth by marrying with some highly rich girl.

When you were at that thought, you see one of your other classmates of the same batch, his wife! You knew that that girl was also having normal financial life. Now you completely in deep thinking and analyzing the complete situation and realizing that this complete set-up is created by your friend only.

Present time, now!

Hey you! Still having some doubt and want to connect another story like he might have won some lottery or hidden treasure in his old house! This is what is contradictory thinking. On one side you also want to have good financial life and on other side creating doubt over doubt on your classmate's financial condition. Still feeling that he might have done some goof-up!

How did our mind work in contradictory feelings?

We all know that our *Subconscious Mind* control over 90 % of our life in each dimension be it a personal, professional, financial, relationship, etc. The subconscious mind is neutral and doesn't understand the logic, like what is right and what is wrong. It understand the feeling and emotions associated with any object or situation.

Like in above examples, how subconscious mind understand the feelings associated with money, on one side you as a person is having a very good feeling about money as you want to be rich but at the same time other contradictory feeling is you are not happy seeing other rich peoples, even you classmate. So subconscious mind will neither consider your positive feeling nor negative feeling about money because of this contradiction.

If this is the case, your subconscious mind will not develop further thought processes on positive feelings about money because as soon as it develops or gives you some idea on how you can acquire a good amount of money, contradictory thoughts pop up and nullify the development.

How to change the situation and improve the financial life?

During this complete episode, somewhere in your mind, you are realizing about your friend that from college time he was very curious about rich people, to understand the process of how they get rich, what is needed in normal person to become rich.

He was having a growth oriented mindset and always keen to learn new things, which can help him to do good in life. Because of these characteristics, from very first semester of graduation, where he had been given grace to pass one subject, eventually, he topped the final semester.

Further, during an interaction at his home, he had narrated some of the key points as meeting with several rich persons all round in his city, talking with them, seeking guidance from them, has helped a lot to change his own thought process. He has started his own small business 15 years back and passionately doing & increasing it to creating wealth.

Key to transformation

He became more and more positive towards rich people, which he once thought that rich peoples might not be co-operative, must have accumulated money with unfair means. Slowly he was realizing that it all starts with a rich mindset to improve one's life. We need to shun all the self-limiting beliefs about rich people and also about money. If we have any ill-feeling about money, money will have an ill-feeling for us! It will be out of your approach in spite of all your efforts.

Rich peoples focus on creating business system, which generate money for them. They solve the problem for mass, thus generate wealth. The level of problem is directly proportional to the level of wealth. If you are making difference in life of *few* people buy your product or service, your earning will be *moderate*. But if you are influencing lives of mass, then you will be millionaire or billionaire.

"A great many years ago, I purchased a fine dictionary. The first thing I did with it was to turn to the word 'impossible,' and neatly clip it out of the book. That would not be an unwise thing for you to do." **– Napoleon Hill**

*****

9. Being Rich is a Right ! – But get rich quick is the myth

Most of us think that being rich is a privilege, there are only a few peoples who can be rich in this world. Even good numbers of the most educated people are firm believers in this thought process. A very less percentage of people think that being rich is a right. We need to follow certain principles for being rich.

Modeling Rich People

Modeling is one of the best ways to become rich in a lifetime. Will you be surprised that people have created more than 100 billion dollar wealth and still growing from scratch? Have you realized this amount? No... Just $ 1 billion is equivalent to > ₹ 7,000 Crore, so $100 billions > ₹ 7,00,000 Crore.

Don't have a belief that all the rich people are bad, it is not at all true. Try to understand the system, they have created to generate money. They have not chased money most of the time, they were behind the idea or solution. The idea which was for solving people's problem, to make their life easy.

Business Prototype to Start with

How they start their journey? They make one small prototype of their business model, test that in all aspects to judge whether that model is making profit or loss. If it's making losses, then what action needs to be taken to avoid those losses. Can we use new technology to bring improvement to the whole process?

If that prototype model is making a profit, then still they continue to improve the profit margins. There are several businesses, in which the company is making unbelievable profit margins.

Once the prototype model is successful, then the real business start. They are able to attract good investors as one can see their physical prototype model. Their business plan is not on paper or on PowerPoint presentations but a real one in the form of a prototype.

I realized in my life that lack of money is not the primary reason for starting any business, it's really the good idea and its execution. If your idea is good, then immediate attention is required to make one real prototype to check the profitability.

Once they(rich people) taste the success, then they take the advantage of leverage, by duplicating the same prototype business model at multiple locations/ outlets.

Get Rich Quick is the Myth!

Most of us want success in life like an event, visualizing winning some awards, achieving something great, but not willing to follow the process which takes you there. We want to win the Olympic Medal, but do not want to do several years of hardship to achieve that. If you want to be the master in any field then you need to gain the domain knowledge of that area & then follow the process to perform to the fullest.

If you want to be rich, then you need to behave like rich, you need to develop certain habits, you need to reflect the rich character, you need to show your passion for your business product or service. And the most important is to 'Start' that process. Unless you start that journey, you will not go anywhere.

It's like you want to cover 1000 miles journey with your car from place X to place Y. The problem is you have just purchased the car and still learning to drive it. So you go ahead, to learn a driving skill which is the foremost requirement. Now what you think that you can reach place Y directly after learning to drive! No, you will not. Next, the very essential step is to *START* the journey from your current place X, then only you will reach place Y. During this journey, you should not be road-focused, you need to be destination-focused.

Accelerate

The main point here is to *start the journey* as early as possible toward your goal. Because only in the way (process) you will be able to learn several things, using them in future you can accelerate.

In business, you will understand when are you making less profit, when are you making a good profit, even when are you making losses. Once you start understanding the whole business process of making a profit and avoiding losses, then you can accelerate things to reach a destination at a pace.

Improvement Oriented Focus

During this journey, you will learn many things a hard way, now how to deal with them for future reference.

Remember, if you take them as a burden on your shoulder, then you are in trouble. It's like some heavyweight on your shoulder, you cannot run with that for long-distance. So, what you really need to do, is to make those learnings stepping stones. You are standing on top of them, and you will use all those learning in your future journey.

Remember, how our subconscious mind (SCM) works, if you keep on thinking about this critical learning all the time, it will serve you much more of a similar kind. But if you make them as a stepping stone, then SCM will help you to achieve your financial goal.

Insightful business message from Autorickshaw-wala

A few years back, I was coming from home town by train. When I reached the station, I hired an autorickshaw to reach my company's residential home. During the journey as a habit, I started talking to the driver, he was from my home state. He shared things like he has not taken the rickshaw on rent but he is the owner of that and he owns a total of two such rickshaws (the other one was with his son).

When I asked him, how much money he is able to earn and similar other questions. He had given clear thought process answers. One very important thing he shared was *"Sahab, duniya main do hi tarah ke dhande hote hain, EK wo; jab aap subah jage, to ho gaya. Aur Doosara wo; jab aapne pure din kam kiya tab hua."* (There are only two types of business in the world, one; when you awake in the morning is done, other; when you work for a full day, then it's done). He had taught me the difference between passive and active income on that day! When your investment/ your money is earning money for you, it's passive income. When you are earning money by directly doing work, then it's active income. You can now realize, which one is better!

"If You Are Born Poor It's Not Your Mistake, But If You Die Poor It's Your Mistake"– Bill Gates

*****

10. Power of Imagination in Financial Success! A proven method to implement

There are several real examples in the world about financial success by the power of imagination. We generally get each thing twice in our life, one while visualizing about it in our mind and then getting that physically. The same is true for your financial accomplishment as well.

You decide your target amount of money, the target date for accomplishment, and what you are willing to sacrifice to achieve that. Now you need to repeat this every day in the morning and evening with full faith. Then slowly this will sink to your subconscious power, which indirectly connected to God, then the miracle happens.

Miracle Happen!

When I was working in rotating shifts in my company somewhere in 2008, one day I got the book in my colleague's room titled 'Think and Grow Rich' by Napoleon Hill. In this book, I like one thought that Hard work is not the key to become rich, if this could have been true, then each labor must have been either millionaire or a billionaire.

I like this thought so much that on next day I bought that book. This thought, wake me up from the inside, because throughout my life, I was having one phenomenon as only hard work is the key to success, be it financial or any other. Most of us get this lesson in our childhood from our elders that with hard work, you can achieve each and everything in life. But the sad fact is it's really not true as you will get tired one day with hardship.

After reading this book, I decided to implement the concept of ***Imagination*** *on myself. I decided to achieve X amount of assets with a target date after three years from that particular date. After following certain principles as stated in this book, I practice them with full faith and reset by old beliefs.*

Truly, after a little more than three years I achieved that decided amount of assets. ***This was not less than a miracle to me.*** From that day onwards, I was clear that a different thought process is required to achieve your financial targets in life.

I am sharing one more real story from this outstanding book in the words of Napoleon Hill on the power of imagination in financial success as below

Power of Imagination (a True Story)!

This story proves the truth of that old saying, "where there's a will, there's a way." It was told to me by that beloved educator and clergyman, the late Frank W. Gunsaulus, who began his preaching career in the stockyards region of South Chicago.

While Dr. Gunsaulus was going through college, he observed many defects in our educational system, defects which he believed he could correct, if he were the head of a college. His deepest desire was to become the directing head of an educational institution in which young men and women would be taught to "learn by doing." He made up his mind to organize a new college in which he could carry out his ideas, without being handicapped by orthodox methods of education.

Need of Million Dollars

He needed a million dollars to put the project across! Where was he to lay his hands on so large a sum of money? That was the question that absorbed most of this ambitious young preacher's thought. But he couldn't seem to make any progress. Every night he took that thought to bed with him. He got up with it in the morning. He took it with him everywhere he went. Then he turned it over and over in his mind until it became a consuming obsession with him.

A million dollars is a lot of money. He recognized that fact, but he also recognized the truth that the only limitation is that which one sets up in one's own mind. Being a philosopher as well as a preacher, Dr. Gunsaulus recognized, as do all who succeed in life, that DEFINITENESS OF PURPOSE is the starting point from which one must begin. He recognized, too, that definiteness of purpose takes on animation, life, and power when backed by a BURNING DESIRE to translate that purpose into its material equivalent.

He knew all these great truths, yet he did not know where, or how to lay his hands on a million dollars. The natural procedure would have been to give up and quit, by saying, "Ah well, my idea is a good one, but I cannot do anything with it, because I never can procure the necessary million dollars." That is exactly what the majority of people would have said, but it is not what Dr. Gunsaulus said.

What he said, and what he did are so important that I now introduce him, and let him speak for himself. "One Saturday afternoon I sat in my room thinking of ways and means of raising the money to carry out my plans. For nearly two years, I had been thinking, but I had done nothing but think! "The time had come for ACTION! "I made up my mind, then and there, that I would get the necessary million dollars within a week. How? I was not concerned about that. The main thing of importance was the decision to get the money within a specified time, and I want to tell you that the moment I reached a definite decision to get the money within a specified time, a strange feeling of assurance came over me, such as I had never before experienced.

Visualization of the Million Dollars

Something inside me seemed to say, 'Why didn't you reach that decision a long time ago? The money was waiting for you all the time!' "Things began to happen in a hurry. I called the newspapers and announced I would preach a sermon the following morning, entitled, 'What I would do if I had a Million Dollars.' "I went to work on the sermon immediately, but I must tell you, frankly, the task was not difficult, because I had been preparing that sermon for almost two years.

The spirit back of it was a part of me! "Long before midnight, I had finished writing the sermon. I went to bed and slept with a feeling of confidence, for I could see myself already in possession of the million dollars. "Next morning I arose early, went into the bathroom, read the sermon, then knelt on my knees and asked that my sermon might come to the attention of someone who would supply the needed money. "While I was praying I again had that feeling of assurance that the money would be forthcoming. In my excitement, I walked out without my sermon and did not discover the oversight until I was in my pulpit and about ready to begin delivering it. "It was too late to go back for my notes, and what a blessing that I couldn't go back!

Instead, my own subconscious mind yielded the material I needed. When I arose to begin my sermon, I closed my eyes and spoke with all my heart and soul of my dreams. I not only talked to my audience, but I fancy I talked also to God. I told what I would do with a million dollars if that amount were placed in my hands. Then I described the plan I had in mind for organizing a great educational institution, where young people would learn to do practical things, and at the same time develop their minds.

Mission Accomplished

"When I had finished and sat down, a man slowly arose from his seat, about three rows from the rear, and made his way toward the pulpit. I wondered what he was going to do. He came into the pulpit, extended his hand, and said, 'Reverend, I liked your sermon. I believe you can do everything you said you would, if you had a million dollars. To prove that I believe in you and your sermon, if you will come to my office tomorrow morning, I will give you the million dollars. My name is Phillip D. Armour.'"

Young Gunsaulus went to Mr. Armour's office and the million dollars was presented to him. With the money, he founded the Armour Institute of Technology. That is more money than the majority of preachers ever see in an entire lifetime, yet the thought impulse back of the money was created in the young preacher's mind in a fraction of a minute. The necessary million dollars came as a result of an idea. Back of the idea was a DESIRE which young Gunsaulus had been nursing in his mind for almost two years.

Observe this important fact . . . HE GOT THE MONEY WITHIN THIRTY-SIX HOURS AFTER HE REACHED A DEFINITE DECISION IN HIS OWN MIND TO GET IT, AND DECIDED UPON A DEFINITE PLAN FOR GETTING IT!

There was nothing new or unique about young Gunsaulus' vague thinking about a million dollars, and weakly hoping for it. Others before him, and many since his time, have had similar thoughts. But there was something very unique and different about the decision he reached on that memorable Saturday, when he put vagueness into the background, and definitely said, "I WILL get that money within a week!" God seems to throw Himself on the side of the man who knows exactly what he wants, if he is determined to get JUST THAT! Moreover, the principle through which Dr. Gunsaulus got his million dollars is still alive!

So have faith in the power of imagination in financial success.

"What is now proved was once only imagined."
— *William Blake*

*****

11. You Can or You Can't (Beliefs)! - Financial dimension of your life

It's your beliefs, which shapes your destiny. Learning how to engage your mind to support growth is the secret of life. Of course, the secret of life is not a secret at all. Several Gurus like Buddha and Jesus have been telling us the same story for ages. ***Several breakthrough research has been done in the last several years on the mind and human psychology.***

Now science is also supporting in the same direction. A human being is not controlled by genes (old thought process) but through beliefs. These beliefs control your lives immensely.

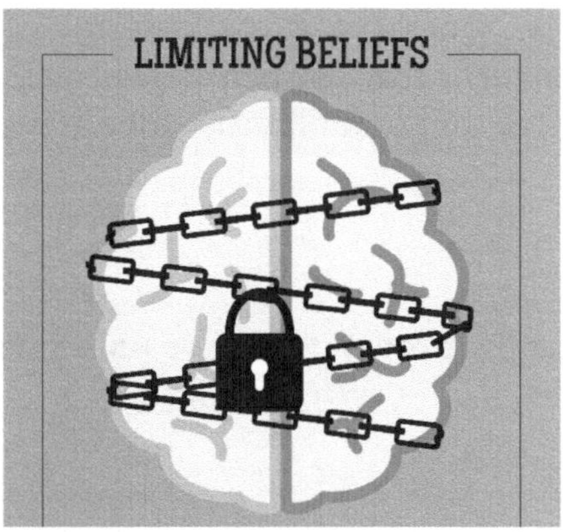

"Your beliefs become your thoughts Your thoughts become your words Your words become your actions Your actions become your habits Your habits become your values Your values become your destiny."- Mahatma Gandhi
It all starts with *BELIEFS* and leads to *DESTINY in the above quote.*

These beliefs, which generally sink in your mind up to the age of seven-year, control 90 % of your life unconsciously.

Many a time these beliefs are false but still, they are powerful enough to control your life. To change these false & limiting beliefs, you need to replace them with more powerful beliefs, which are true, based on scientific facts & researches.

These beliefs affect each dimension of our life, be it personal, professional, spiritual, social, financial, etc. As there are so many dimensions, so we are going to discuss financial life here.

Because financial life is one, by which each and every other dimension is connected. I hope most of you will agree with me. We cannot pay out electricity bills, children education fee by some spiritual means, we need money for that.

One of my life's mission is to bring changes in the financial lives of millions of people by changing their false & limiting beliefs about money. And I hope you are with me to change your own life and at the same time to spread these factful messages to your friends and loved ones.

How do we take actions based on Beliefs!

You are planning to buy a car. If you are feeling that your next car will be a low-cost car, then you are having one set of thought processes. But if you are feeling for the high-cost car, then you are in a different set of thought processes.

Actually, peoples do their buying much before in mind than to get that product physically. The following can be the thought process scenarios in your mind-

Scenario 1: Cash is not the concern, then you will simply go to a car showroom and purchase your car as per your choice. Be it low cost, medium cost, or high cost.

Scenario 2: If you are having a limited budget & in your family purchasing only a new product is preferred, then the situation may be different. Though you are wishing to have a good car, but you'll go for the low-cost car.

Scenario 3: Budget is limited, but a good second-hand car is not at all a discussion point in your family, then you can have that. You are not wishing to have a second-hand car, but due to budget limitations, you are making that decision. Later, once you have a sufficient budget you will definitely go for a new high-cost car.

Scenario 4: Not having sufficient funds this time, but want to have a good car and only a new one. Now in this case you will either increase your earning means or simply follow the loan system. But remember, the loan is good for asset purchasing not for liability purchase.

So, what am I saying here is there are always multiple-choice to approach in any situation. In some choices, we play safe and within our comfort zone, and in others, we cross our comfort boundary.

<u>Not all time-rich people buy the new products!</u>

One of my colleagues was from a highly rich family, whenever I talk to him, I wonder why is he doing the job. He used to come by different bikes or cars to the company from very early days.

One day he came with a beautiful superbike. On that day he receives a lot of greetings as his bike was having stunning look. Later one day, I ask him the cost of that bike. He said it cost him around ₹ 9 lakhs. Another day I was searching for that bike on google, I found that cost around ₹ 19 lakhs. It was a bit surprising, how can that person was not telling the correct price.

After few days, I shared with him about my google search, he smiled and said, 'though my bike looks like just arriving from the showroom, but I purchased that second hand'.

Make better choices for financial life

As we are having multiple options to act in any given situation. How we make final choices is driven by our beliefs and the environment we live in.

Majority time we act like our parents or guardian who is having a good influence on us. If we have seen most of our relatives or friends buying cars using loans, then quite a good chance that we shall go with loan options.

But if we have seen them as a business creator, from which money pouring regularly, then we shall soon be like them only.

We many time limits ourselves to grow financially in spite of knowing the fact that there is several thousand self-made millionaires in the world. Also across the world, out of total billionaires, more than 70 % of billionaires are self-made ($1 billion > ₹7000 crore).

My trading experience of beliefs!

So, the point is we need to shun limiting beliefs about money and replacing them with abundance beliefs. I personally used this for trading for around 4.5 months. Before starting trading, I asked some of my friends that what is their net portfolio, the answer was that in some shares there is very good or good profit and in others it is loss. Overall hardly one or two who were having their portfolio in positive.

Before starring, I mentally prepared myself that I shall only make a profit in trading. I asked good practices to some of the people, who were doing good in trading. A few of them given some personal advice and also suggested weekly magazines for trading. Believe me friends, during that period, my portfolio was always on the positive side. Later I sold most of my stocks and invested that money in another stream.

Overall it's your mind, which acts as per your beliefs, your thought processes. It's subconscious power is so powerful that it can turn any dimension of your life into heaven or hell. So keep feeding good thoughts, positive thoughts, abundance thought to mind always, it's subconscious power will reflect the same in reality.

"If a hundred-foot oak tree had the mind of a human, it would only grow to be ten feet tall!"
- T. Harv Eker

*****

12. Beliefs which differentiate Rich People! - Understand them all for success

Becoming world-class rich is not easy for middle-class people. Some of them understand the logic of being rich and put effort to jump from middle class to world-class. But during this time, the financial scale changes across the world, and they remain in the middle class only. The gap either remains the same or widens between world-class and middle-class people.

Here we shall understand some of the universal laws about rich people thinking. How they think about money, about other rich people, about creating wealth. Credit to *Steve Siebold,* a self-made multi-millionaire, for his research for 30 years on this topic by interviewing more than 1,200 of the world's wealthiest people.

<u>Money is simple (not complicated)</u>

While a very large size of the population believes that money is complicated, but rich people think that money flows from the idea! They know the more value they create in the marketplace the wealthier they will become. We can call them the master of solving people's problems and then generating wealth in return. They attract money because they are problem solvers. The bigger the solution, the bigger the paycheck. It's that simple.

The masses have always thought that rich people are smarter, luckier, or more educated. Of course, none of these things is true. The rich see making money through the eyes of endless possibilities and aren't afraid to stake their claim. No matter how often they fail, they persist until they got the success. Their mindset is rooted in the abundant potential every new idea presents, and they live in a consciousness full of excitement and grand anticipation of results.

So while the middle class approaches money with the mind of an over academic angle, the rich people approach money like a child who doesn't understand lack and limitation. They do not believe in limitations.

Middle class and lower middle class are happy in what they have but world-class has a growth mindset. And with that mindset, they create millions, billions. Making money may not be easy, but it is simple. There is no mystery to getting rich, but this limiting belief stops most people from ever trying.

Rich People are Ambitious (Not Crooks)

The average person has been programmed in childhood by well-meaning parents, teachers, coaches, clergy, and others of influence to believe rich people acquire wealth through dishonesty and cheating. This is one of the excuses the masses use to justify a lack of financial success.

World-class thinkers know the majority of fortunes were built through ambition, drive, and vision. Off course there may be some crooks among rich people but it's true in middle and lower group also. So this excuse of the middle class is not at all true. This group generally does not take full responsibility for its result. They think that they are not financially well because of rich people.

Unfortunately, they often pass these misrepresentations onto their children, and the belief carries on growing stronger with each generation. Meanwhile, the world-class takes full responsibility for their own results and directs their mental energy towards getting rich. Instead of wasting their brain power on excuses, they use it to harness their creativity and solve bigger problems.

While the masses use the latest scandal to prove their argument against the rich, millionaires are hard at work thinking of new ideas. One group focuses on excuses and blame, the other, on taking action and getting results. Is it any wonder that the middle class is broke and the world-class is rich? The ambition of the self-made rich individual comes from self-confidence and an ability to use thought and perseverance to get what they want.

Believes in Team Effort (Not solitary)

The average person clocks in at nine and out at five. They are paid for the results of their individual efforts. This limits what they're worth to an organization. Rich people know it takes a team to build wealth, and they focus much of their effort on finding the right people to leverage their actions and ideas.

The greatest fortunes are built through the collective mental and physical contributions of a world-class team. The rich see themselves as team leaders, whether their teams consist of employees, partners, or outsourced contractors. They assemble their team and carefully orchestrate each move the team makes according to a well-planned strategy.

While the masses are interested in getting personal credit for the results they achieve, the great ones happily give the credit to their teams and prefer to trade personal recognition for profit. So as the middle class proudly displays their ribbons, trophies, and gold watches, the world-class sees their reward as growing net worth.

One group is content to be comfortable, and the other is content to be rich. And one of the primary differences rests in the rich's willingness and ability to build a team and share the credit. Since the masses don't make much money, they crave recognition. The masses are more ego-focused than results-oriented.

Dreams about money (Not worries)

The average person spends an extravagant amount of time worrying about money while simultaneously denying its significance. The masses are conditioned in childhood to repeat the phrase; "I don't care about money."

Rich people bund such limiting belief at an early stage and focus on acquiring their fortune, oftentimes for the sole purpose of not having to worry about it. After earning their fortunes, many of them continue working because they love what they do. It's rarely about amassing more silver and gold because the newly rich learn there are limits to what money can do.

While the masses mentally have thoughts of fear and scarcity, the rich are operating in a mindset of love, abundance, and endless possibility. The absence of fear allows them to see life and business as a game, and their financial success serves with their confidence.

Superior intelligence and higher education are not the secrets to their success, but the early adoption of a world-class set of beliefs and philosophies are. These values serve their best interests and move them towards their goals and dreams. The great ones dream about money and acquire it so they can move on to more important pursuits. They always believe in the realization of their greatest potential.

Way ahead

Remember, you cannot be rich unless your start thinking positively about money & rich people. If you have contradictory thoughts about money then it will be away from you in life. In case of contradiction, your subconscious power does not develop good things for you in any area of life.

So change your self-limiting beliefs about money to abundance. Nurture and cherish them with positive feelings then a miracle will happen in your financial life.

"Rich people have small TVs and big libraries, and poor people have small libraries and big TVs."

– *Zig Ziglar*

*****

13. Money.... Negative or Positive? Your opinion matters a lot!

Money is negative or positive? What is opinion? If you think that money is positive, I can bet, you are doing good in your financial life. But if you think that money is negative, then wait for the moment and just analyze your financial life. What is the condition? All is well! I guess...It's not, you are struggling in your financial life.

Most people have an ill feelings about money, they see it as a negative thing in their life. They know it is very important to have it but do not give much focus.

Steve Siebold had done research on the thinking of the masses and rich people for several years. How most of people & rich people think differently about money, money's connection with formal education & How money can be earned.

Thinking (*about* Money)

"Ask most people about money and you'll understand why they don't have any. The masses see ambitious people as greedy and self-serving. They see money as a necessary evil that must be managed but never focused on. After all, there are more righteous pursuits, like television, sports, and movies. The idea of building wealth seems shallow. It also seems like a lot of work.

The rich see money as a positive tool that has the power to create freedom and opportunity for themselves and their families. Being wealthy gives them the option to live what author/philosopher Ayn Rand called "an unrestricted existence."

This means having the ability to do what they want, when they want, with whom they want, for as long as they want, without limitations. It also gives them the freedom to engage in their favorite pastimes, no matter how lavish or seemingly impractical to the masses.

Many millionaires form charitable foundations and donate substantial sums to the less fortunate. Without the ongoing support of wealthy benefactors, most charities would not survive. So while the middle class demonizes and criticizes the world class for selfishness and greed, the latter is donating a lion's share of the money that keeps charities alive.

Many also pay more taxes in a year than most people pay in a lifetime, and are essentially responsible for funding the infrastructure of the government's tax base. At the heart of this level of thinking is the belief that money is either a tool of evil or empowerment. The belief you adopt will lead you to abundant wealth or middle-class mediocrity."

Thinking (*about* Education & Money)

"While the rich respect the power of formal education, they usually don't associate it with building a financial empire. Many world-class performers have little formal education and have amassed their wealth through the acquisition and subsequent sale of specific knowledge.

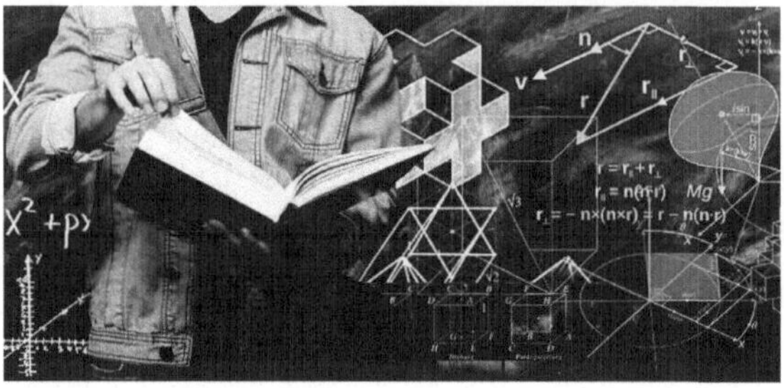

Formal education teaches people how to think and perform in the linear world of commerce, but the rich rarely become wealthy trading time for money. The great ones operate from a non-linear mindset that keeps them perpetually in the consciousness of creative thought. At this elevated level of thinking, there are no limits or boundaries, and the sole focus is on solving the seemingly unsolvable.

In this nonlinear school of thought, two and two no longer equal four, and anything is possible. The rich use their brainpower in addition to the brainpower of others to hone in on ultra-specific solutions their competitors have given up on.

Meanwhile, the masses are convinced that master's degrees and doctorates are the way to wealth, mostly because they are trapped in the linear line of thought that holds them back from higher levels of consciousness.

One of the greatest secrets of the rich lies in their ability to rely on their common sense and a street-smart approach to problem-solving. While the middle class makes simple problems seem complex, the world-class makes complex problems seem simple. Their ability to reduce any problem to an elementary level allows them to see solutions most academics wouldn't even consider.

The wealthy aren't interested in the means, only the end. Solve the problem, get compensated, and repeat the process until you're rich. End of story. This single-minded focus always pays off sooner or later, at which time the masses will call it luck."

Thinking (*about* How to Earn Money)

"The average person believes the harder they work the more money they'll make. Their linear thinking equates labor and effort with financial success. This is why most people aren't rich. They're following an outdated model of success and are confounded when they reach middle age with little money to show for twenty years of hard work.

The rich know that creative thinking is the highest-paid skill in the world. Independent, creative thinking is the most valuable asset anyone can acquire. So while the masses are trying to figure out how to put their kids through college and retire on half of what they can barely exist on now, the great ones are building empires, living in abundance, and donating large sums to their favorite causes.

This sets off a psychological domino effect because once a person thinks and lives at this level of abundance, they know even greater levels of success are possible through the vehicle of creative thought. Most of us were told as kids that if we paid attention in school, got good grades, and went to a respectable college or university, our success was virtually guaranteed.

The reality is few people who follow this formula ever get rich. They survive, and some become the most successful people in their families. But world-class wealth is rarely achieved by people who follow this model. The rich eventually figure out that training your mind to find solutions to difficult problems is the real secret to making money.

The good news is this is possible for anyone who conditions their mind to think this way, and then transforms thought into action."

Way ahead!

So if your financial condition is not appreciable, then you need to start thinking differently. Switching over to a new thinking pattern may take some time but you will get a good result. You can make a list of your self-limiting beliefs about money and also about other things associated with money.

Analyze these beliefs and develop new & more powerful money-associated beliefs. Keep on repeating these new beliefs in your daily routine, till they get absorbed in your mind, your subconscious mind. Believe me, once you are having a positive feeling about money, about rich people, things will start changing in your life.

In the majority of cases, it's boiled down to one point, rich peoples are masters of solving the problems of the masses. In return for their solution, they get a substantial return.

"Formal education will make you a living. Self-education will make you a fortune."- **Jim Rohn**

*****

14. Think, Act and Grow Rich - Financial journey begins with one thought!

Think, Act, and Grow Rich! Thinking rather hard work is the first and foremost requirement in your journey towards richness. Whoever you are—regardless of your age, your education, or your occupation—you can attract wealth. Your positive belief about wealth will bring you wealth but at the same time, any negative belief about wealth will keep you in the same condition for a long time or lifetime.

It all starts with one thought at any moment of time in your life. If your start taking action based on that thought you can soon attain the path of wealth. Below is one real story about a person, who was admitted to the hospital. He had started reading one book there and began his journey towards richness. *(Credit to book 'Success Through a Positive Mental Attitude' by Napoleon Hill and W. Clement Stone)*

Trigger Point at Hospital Bed!

Time after time as we have studied the careers of successful men, we have discovered that they date their own success from the day they picked up a self-improvement book. Never underestimate the value of a book. Books are tools, providing inspiration that can launch you onto a bold new program and which can also light the dark days that any such program entails.

George Stefek was recovering at the Veterans Administration Hospital in Hines, Illinois. There he discovered by accident the value of thinking time. Financially—he was broke. While George was convalescing, he had a great deal of time on his hands. There wasn't too much to do except read and think. He read *Think and Grow Rich.* And he was ready.

Business Idea

An idea occurred to him. Many laundries, George knew, fold their newly ironed shirts over a piece of cardboard to keep the shirts stiff and free from wrinkles. By writing a few letters, George learned that these shirt boards cost the laundries about $4.00 per thousand. His idea was to sell the boards for $1.00 a thousand; however, each one would carry an advertisement. The advertisers would, of course, pay for space, and George would make a profit.

Execution Begin

George had an idea and he tried to make it work. When he left the hospital, he got into action!

New in the advertising field, he had his problems. But he finally developed successful sales techniques through what others term "trial and error" and we term "trial and success."

George continued the custom he had started in the hospital to engage in study, thinking, and planning time each day.

Even when George's business was moving ahead swiftly, he decided to increase his sales by increasing the efficiency of his service. The shirt boards, when withdrawn from the shirts, were not retained by the laundries' customers.

Good Question#1 for Growth

Now, he asked himself the question: "How can I get families to keep these shirt boards with the advertisements on them?" The solution flashed into his mind.

What did he do? On one side of the shirt board, he continued to print an advertisement in black and white or in colors. On the other side, he added something new—an interesting game for the children, a delicious recipe for the wife, or a provocative crossword puzzle for the whole family. George tells about one husband who complained that his laundry bill had gone up in a sudden, unaccountable way. Then he discovered that his wife was sending in shirts to the laundry which ordinarily he could have worn another day, just to get more of George's recipes!

Good Question#2 for Growth

But George didn't stop there. He was ambitious. He wanted to expand his business still further. Again he asked himself the question: "How?" And he found the answer.

George Stefek gave the entire $1.00 per thousand he received from the laundries to the American Institute of Laundering. The Institute, in turn, recommended that each member help himself and his trade association by using George Stefek's shirt boards exclusively.

Important Discovery

And thus George made another important discovery: *the more you give of that which is good and desirable—the more you get!*

Now a carefully planned thinking time session brought George Stefek considerable wealth. He discovered that a time apart is essential to any successful attraction of riches.

It is in quiet that our best ideas occur to us. Don't make the mistake of believing that by a frantic kind of dashing around you are being your most effective and efficient self. Don't assume that you are wasting time when you take time out for thought. The thought is the foundation upon which all else is built by man to grow rich.

<u>Way Ahead</u>

Now it isn't necessary for you to go to a hospital to establish the habit of reading good motivating books, to think or to make plans. And your thinking, study, and planning sessions need not be too lengthy. If you invest only one percent of your time in a study, thinking, and planning session it will make an amazing difference in the speed with which you reach your goals.

Your day has 1,440 minutes in it. Invest one percent of that time in a study, thinking, and planning session. And you will be astounded at what those fourteen minutes do for you. For it may surprise you to find that when you develop this habit you will receive constructive ideas almost any time or anywhere you might be: while doing the dishes, or riding the bus, or while taking a bath. This is the power of your subconscious mind.

Be certain to use two of the greatest, yet simplest working tools ever invented – tools used by a genius like <u>Thomas Edison</u> – a pencil and a piece of paper. For he always had handy – paper and pencil. And thus you, like him, will record the ideas that come to you day or night.

Another requirement to attract wealth is to learn how to set your goal. Across the world, less than 5 % of people have written financial goals for themselves, and most of the time they grow rich. Our mind has tremendous power to develop the thought process to initiate actions to achieve those goals. Remember, nothing moves in life without actions.

Set your mind on a definite goal and observe how quickly the world stands aside to let you pass.
— *Napoleon Hill*

*****

15. The Richest Man in Babylon - A proven secret to grow rich!

The Richest Man in Babylon is a 1926 book by George S. Clason that dispenses financial advice through a collection of parables set 4,000 years ago in ancient Babylon. The book remains in print almost a century after the parables were originally published, and is regarded as a classic of personal financial advice.

The parables are told by a fictional Babylonian character called Arkad, a poor scribe who became the "richest man in Babylon". Included in Arkad's advice are the "Seven Cures" (or how to generate money and wealth), and the "Five Laws of Gold" (or how to protect and invest wealth).

Far and wide, Arkad was famed for his great wealth. Also, was he famed for his liberality. He was generous in his charities and with his family. He was liberal in his own expenses. But nevertheless each year his wealth increased more rapidly than he spent it.

And there were certain friends of younger days who came to him and said: "You, Arkad, are more fortunate than we. You have become the richest man in all Babylon while we struggle for existence. You can wear the finest garments and you can enjoy the rarest foods, while we must be content if we can clothe our families in raiment that is presentable and feed them as best we can.

Equal Opportunity

"Yet, once we were equal. We studied under the same master. We played the same games. And in neither the studies nor the games did you outshine us. And in the years since, you have been no more an honorable citizen than we.

"Nor have you worked harder or more faithfully, insofar as we can judge. Why, then, should a fickle fate single you out to enjoy all the good things of life and ignore us who are equally deserving?"

Thereupon Arkad remonstrated with them, saying, "If you have not acquired more than a bare existence in the years since we were youths, it is because you either have failed to learn the laws that govern the building of wealth, or else you do not observe them.

Curious to Know 'How'

His friends appeal to him to explain to them how he had become possessed of so much prosperity, so he continued: "In my youth, I looked about me and saw all the good things there were to bring happiness and contentment. And I realized that wealth increased the potency of all these. "Wealth is power. With wealth many things are possible.

"One may ornament the home with the richest of furnishings, sail the distant seas, feast on the delicacies of far lands. "One may buy the ornaments of the gold worker and the stone polisher, even build mighty temples for the gods.

The decision to Accumulate Wealth

"And, when I realized all this, I decided to myself that I would claim my share of the good things of life. I would not be one of those who stand afar off, enviously watching others enjoy. Also, I would not be content to clothe myself in the cheapest raiment that looked respectable and would not be satisfied with the lot of a poor man. On the contrary, I would make myself a guest at this banquet of good things.

"Being, as you know, the son of a humble merchant, one of a large family with no hope of an inheritance, and not being endowed, as you have so frankly said, with superior powers or wisdom, I decided that if I was to achieve what I desired, time and study would be required.

"As for time, all men have it in abundance. You, each of you, have let slip by sufficient time to have made yourselves wealthy. Yet, you admit; you have nothing to show except your good families, of which you can be justly proud.

"As for the study, did not our wise teacher teach us that learning was of two kinds: the one kind being the things we learned and knew, and the other being the training that taught us how to find out what we did not know?

"Therefore did I decide to find out how one might accumulate wealth, and when I had found out, to make this my task and do it well. For, is it not wise that we should enjoy while we dwell in the brightness of the sunshine, for sorrows enough shall descend upon us when we depart for the darkness of the world of spirit?

Got the Mentor!

"I found employment as a scribe in the hall of records, and long hours each day I labored upon the clay tablets. Week after week, and month after month, I labored, yet for my earnings, I had naught to show. Food and clothing and penance to the gods, and other things of which I could remember not what, absorbed all my earnings. But my determination did not leave me.

"And one-day Algamish, the moneylender, came to the house of the city master and ordered a copy of the Ninth Law, and he said to me, I must have this in two days, and if the task is done by that time, two coppers will I give to thee."

"So I labored hard, but the law was long, and when Algamish returned the task was unfinished. He was angry and had I been his slave, he would have beaten me. But knowing the city master would not permit him to injure me, I was unafraid, so I said to him, 'Algamish, you are a very rich man. Tell me how I may also become rich, and all night I will carve upon the clay, and when the sun rises it shall be completed.'

"He smiled at me and replied, 'You are a forward knave, but we will call it a bargain.'

"All that night I carved, though my back pained and the smell of the wick made my headache until my eyes could hardly see. But when he returned at sunup, the tablets were complete.

'Now,' I said, 'tell me what you promised.'

<u>Secret Revealed</u>

'You have fulfilled your part of our bargain, my son,' he said to me kindly, 'and I am ready to fulfill mine. I will tell you these things you wish to know because I am becoming an old man, and an old tongue loves to wag. And when a youth comes to age for advice he receives the wisdom of years. But too often does youth think that age knows only the wisdom of days that are gone, and therefore profits not.

'Mark you well my words, for if you do not you will fail to grasp the truth that I will tell you, and you will think that your night's work has been in vain.'

"Then he looked at me shrewdly from under his shaggy brows and said in a low, forceful tone, 'I found the road to wealth when I decided that a part of all I earned was mine to keep. And so will you.'

"Then he continued to look at me with a glance that I could feel pierce me but said no more.

'Is that all?' I asked.

'That was sufficient to change the heart of a sheepherder into the heart of a money lender,' he replied.

'But all I earn is mine to keep, is it not?' I demanded.

'Far from it,' he replied. 'Do you not pay the garment-maker? Do you not pay the sandal-maker? Do you not pay for the things you eat? Can you live in Babylon without spending? What have you shown for your earnings for the past month? What for the past year? Fool! You pay to everyone but yourself. Dullard, you labor for others. As well be a slave and work for what your master gives you to eat and wear. If you did keep for yourself one-tenth of all you earn, how much would you have in ten years?'

"My knowledge of the numbers did not forsake me, and I answered, 'As much as I earn in one year.'

Pay yourself First

'You speak but half the truth,' he retorted. *'Every gold piece you save is a slave to work for you. Every copper it earns is its child that also can earn for you. If you would become wealthy, then what you save must earn, and its children must earn, that all may help to give to you the abundance you crave.'*

'You think I cheat you for your long night's work,' he continued, 'but I am paying you a thousand times over if you have the intelligence to grasp the truth I offer you.

Men of action are favoured by the goddess of good luck-
George S. Clason

*****

16. Money....Finite or Infinite Resource! What do you think & believe?

Thinking of rich people keeps them apart from the middle class. Both these classes think about money most of the time but in a different contexts. The middle class thinks of money as a scarce resource but at the same time rich and world-class thinks of money as an abundant resource. There are plenty of problems in the world. Rich people think about solutions to these problems and thus the intern becomes richer.

Steve Siebold has interviewed several rich and world-class people for more than 20 years. Some of the key highlights of his work on how rich people and middle-class people think about money. Here your subconscious mind plays a big role. Once you set the rich people thought process, it keeps on feeding you such input continuously. And during this process, your financial life also improves.

Spending or Investing Thought Process

The middle class is famous for living beyond their means. They're not spendthrifts, but they earn so little they have to spend it all in order to live a decent existence. To further exacerbate their frustration, they're scolded by financial experts who insist they discipline themselves and trim their spending. This is sound but middle-class advice.

The world-class answer is to double or triple your income and create enough wealth so you can enjoy the good life to your heart's desire without worries. This way, you can join the wealthy and focus on investing the remainder of your money in stocks, bonds, real estate, art, and any other wealth-building vehicle you choose. The rich get richer because they know the world is overflowing with wealth disguised as problems that need to be solved.

They know any free-market economy will gladly make them as rich as they desire in exchange for solutions to problems. The bigger problems you solve, the wealthier society will make you. The more people who benefit from your ideas, the more abundance you receive in return. The more you have to invest, the more your money goes to work for you, even as you sleep. That's another reason the rich get richer: they've learned how to make money work for them twenty-four hours a day. So instead of focusing on spending and saving, focus on how to earn more, invest a percentage, and spend the remainder any way you wish.

Emotional or Logical View of Money

Most people never accumulate much money due to a series of self-limiting beliefs around the subject fueled by negative emotions. By the time the average person becomes an adult, they've been brainwashed with dozens of middle-class beliefs and philosophies about money which virtually guarantees them a life of financial mediocrity.

Children, teenagers, and young adults hear negative money messages over and over until they become beliefs that dictate their behavior. In short, a middle-class thinker can't teach you how to become a world-class thinker. A poor person can't teach you how to get rich. These statements are obvious to any rational-thinking person operating from a logic-based mindset. Few people are able to think about money without clouding the subject with negative emotion, which is generated from dozens of middle-class beliefs. An ordinarily smart, well-educated, and otherwise successful person can be instantly transformed into a fear-based, scarcity-driven thinker whose greatest financial aspiration is to retire comfortably.

The world-class sees money for what it is and what it's not, through the eyes of logic. The great ones know money is a critical tool that presents options and opportunities. They also know if you're not happy without it you won't be happy with it. When it comes to thinking about money, put your emotions on the shelf and let reason be your guide.

Pleasurable or Money-Oriented Action

The masses spend a substantial amount of time entertaining themselves in a variety of activities. They live in a state of consciousness where effort is minimal and pleasure is king. Billion-dollar industries are created overnight when smart marketers give the masses what they want most: comfort and entertainment.

Rich people focus the majority of their attention on money-making activities they enjoy. Wealthy people know leverage is one of the great secrets of success, and they go to great lengths to employ it. While the masses are memorizing box scores and batting averages, the world-class is directing the same amount of mental energy into revenue-producing ideas. To the average person, it looks like the rich are working all the time, but one of the smartest strategies of the world class is doing what they love and finding a way to get paid for it. The world-class is famous for saying the best thing about being rich is you never have to do anything you don't want to do, and this includes how they earn money.

The critical thinking question is which comes first; doing what you love or making money to ensure you have the choice? While either way will work, the majority of wealthy people Steve Siebold has interviewed over the past 26 years didn't make serious money until they were doing what they loved. Over and over they've told you the same thing: when you're doing what you love, you think about it 24 hours a day.

Money a Finite or Infinite Resource

The average person believes there's a limited amount of money, and that they need to struggle and fight for their share before someone else gets it. They live in a world of fear and scarcity that says money is hard to make and harder to keep. Due to years of middle-class programming, their negative and limiting relationship with money almost guarantees they will never accumulate more than a modest net worth.

Once again, the rich occupy the opposite side of the spectrum. Although most of them had the same middle-class, fear-based programming in childhood, somewhere along the way they were able to reprogram their beliefs and develop a healthy relationship with money. The rich understand money flows from ideas, and since ideas are limitless, money is limitless. So while the masses are directing their mental energy toward grabbing as much money as they can, the great ones are focused on creating new ideas that have the potential of generating abundant wealth. Rich people use the money to fuel their passions and bring their dreams to life.

The middle class has always criticized the world class for being greedy, ruthless, and materialistic, and there is a segment of successful people that fits this description, known as the upper class. These people are driven by blind ambition and killer instinct. If you get in their way, they will run you over without hesitation.

But the world-class is different. The world-class is spirit-centered, and they are among the most caring, compassionate people. These are the folks who provide the majority of the funding for great charities and non-profit causes. The reason they aren't afraid to give is they know money is in infinite supply. If they need more, they simply use their mind to create more.

***The truth is you have to have great ideas that solve problems to make money. If you do, you will attract money like a magnet.* - Steve Siebold**

******

17. Habit of Saving Money! - Way towards living a prosperous life

Habits play a vital role in saving and investing money, thus making an individual's life prosperous. In general, peoples correlate habits only with non-financial aspects of life, which is only a half-truth.

We all know that saving money is very essential to manage various financial aspects of our life. Saying is easy than doing. Advising one to save money without describing how to save would be somewhat like drawing a picture of a horse and writing under it, "This is a horse." It is obvious to all that saving money is one of the essentials for success, but the big question uppermost in the minds of the majority of those who do not save is: *"How to do it?"*

Saving money is solely a matter of habit.

It is literally true that man, through habit, shapes his own personality. Through repetition, any act in a few times becomes a habit, and the mind appears to be nothing more than a mass of motivating forces growing out of our daily habits.

When once fixed in the mind a habit voluntarily urges one to action. For example, follow a given route to your daily work, or to some other place that you frequently visit, and very soon the habit has been formed and your mind will lead you over that route without thought on your part. Moreover, if you start out with the intention of traveling in another direction, without keeping the thought of the change in routes constantly in mind, you will find yourself following the old route.

Public speakers have found that the telling over and over again of a story, which may be based upon pure fiction, brings into play the role of habit, and very soon they forget whether -the story is true or not.

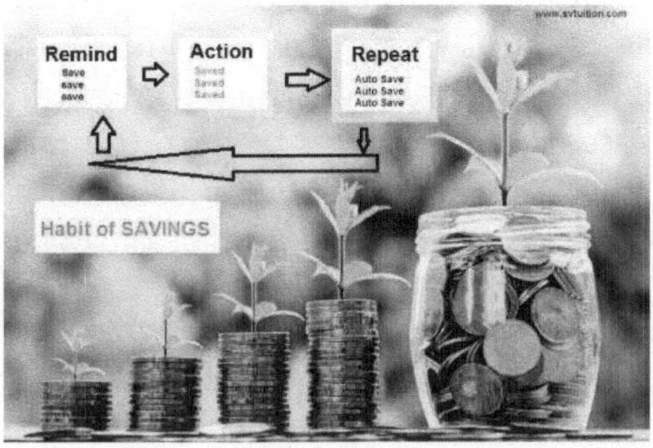

Effect of Habits (Poverty or Prosperity)

The majority of people go through life in poverty and want because they have made destructive use of their habits. Those who remain in poverty seldom realize that they are where they are as the result of their own acts and habits play a very important part in that.

Put in your mind the thought that your ability is limited to a given earning capacity and you will never earn more than that. By continuously having this thought in mind, it will set up a definite limitation of the amount you can earn, and your subconscious mind will accept this limitation. Once your subconscious mind accepts this limitation, the opportunity will no longer knock at your door. You will live in fear of poverty; your doom will be sealed.

Formation of the habit of saving does not mean that you shall limit your earning capacity; it means just the opposite. The habit of saving will not only conserve the amount you earn, in a systematic manner, but it also places you in the way of greater opportunity and gives you the vision, self-confidence, imagination, enthusiasm, initiative, and leadership actually to increase your earning capacity.

Action plan

Set a definite chief aim for yourself, in your mind, an accurate, definite description of that which you want, including the amount of money you intend to earn. Your subconscious mind takes over this picture that you have created and uses it as a blueprint, chart, or map by which to mold your thoughts and actions into practical plans for attaining the object of your chief aim, or purpose.

Through habit, you keep the object of your definite chief aim fixed in your mind until it becomes firmly and permanently implanted there. This practice will destroy the poverty consciousness and set up, in its place, a prosperity consciousness. You will actually begin to demand prosperity, you will begin to expect it, you will begin to prepare yourself to receive it.

Once the above becomes a permanent thought process through the power of habit, focus more on increasing your earning power. As your earnings increase, your savings will, likewise, increase in proportion.

By ever urging yourself on and demanding of yourself increased earning power, on the one hand, and by systematically laying aside a definite amount of all your earnings, on the other hand, you will soon reach the point at which you have removed all imaginary limitations from your own mind and you will then be well started on the road toward financial independence. (Source: book 'Law of Success' by Napoleon Hill)Major Advantages

 # Managing Emergencies:

As the name suggested emergencies are always unexpected. Saving in the form of *No Udhari (Borrow) Fund* helps here. You do not fall into the trap of debt, by borrowing from friends, relatives, and banks.

 # Situation of job loss:

Job loss is usually traumatic. It can leave an individual as well as a family in a huge crisis. Saving can be a great support at the time of job loss.

 # Create Investment opportunities:

Saving creates great opportunities for investment. Many a time such opportunities strike and can be availed with a minimal investment amount like buying shares when there is a steep fall in the share market. If you have savings, you can make fortune at that time.

 # Managing down payment for a mortgage:

Any financial institution asks for a down payment of a certain percentage before the loan is approved. Many a time I have seen people taking a personal loan to manage this down payment as they are not having saving in place.

 # More comfortable in retirement:

Unless one is having the habit of saving and investing, it will be very difficult to retire in peace. I have seen people working at very old age as they are having a constant fear of being broke if they stop working. One more probable reason here is debt becomes a permanent part of their life.

 # Less or no use of Credit Card:

You can avoid the trend of purchasing each and every item through a credit card. If you are not disciplined enough on the timely payment of credit cards, then you are inviting trouble. The interest rates are skyrocketing after the payment due date even if you pay the minimum amount as stated in your credit card bill.

Do not save what is left after spending, but spend what is left after saving. – Warren Buffett

18. Wealth Files - Don't wish but commit to become rich !

Wealth files reveal the secret of 'how can one become rich'. If you take public opinion on 'whether people want to be rich'. They'll look at you as if you were crazy. "Of course, I want to be rich," they'll say. The truth, however, is that most people don't really want to be rich. Why? Because they have a lot of negative <u>beliefs</u> about wealth in their subconscious mind that tells them there is something wrong with being rich. (*Image credit-pixabay*)

<u>What is Your Response?</u>

If we further drill down on '*What are the possible negative beliefs about being rich or trying to get rich?*' Below is the type of response we get from various people.

"Being rich is the right to only a few people. I am not part of that group"

"Rich people are not happy"

"Rich people are selfish and greedy. I really do not want to do any of that....means I do not want to be rich"

"What if I make it and lose it? Then I'll really be a failure."

"I'll never know if people like me for myself or for my money."

"I'll be in the highest tax bracket and have to give half my money to the government."

"It's too much work."

"I could lose my health trying."

"I could be robbed." "My kids could be kidnapped."

"It's too much responsibility. I'll have to manage all that money. I'll have to really understand investments."

"I have to hire expensive accountants and lawyers."

And on and on it goes....

Positive + Negative = Neutral Result

We have both types of beliefs about money in our mind. Positive beliefs about wealth include why being rich would be wonderful. However, for many people, associated negative belief includes information as to why being rich might not be so wonderful. This means they have mixed internal messages about wealth. One part of them joyfully says, "Having more money will make life a lot more fun." But then another part screams, "Yeah, but I'm going to have to work like a dog! What fun is that?" This type of mixed message may seem innocent enough, but in reality, they are one of the major reasons most people never become rich.

You can look at it like this. The universe, which is another way of saying "higher power," is akin to a big mail-order department. It is constantly delivering people, events, and things to you. You "order" what you get by sending energetic messages out to the universe based on your predominant beliefs. Again, based on the Law of Attraction, the universe will do its best to say yes and support you. But if you have mixed messages in your file, the universe can't understand what you want.

One minute the universe hears that you want to be rich, so it begins sending you opportunities for wealth. But then it hears you say, "Rich people are greedy," so the universe begins to support you in not having much money. But then you think, "Having a lot of money makes life so much more enjoyable," so the poor universe, confused, restarts sending you opportunities for more money. The next day you're in an uninspired mood so you think, "Money's not that important." The frustrated universe finally screams, "Make up your final mind! I'll get you what you want, just tell me what it is!"

The number one reason most people don't get what they want is that they don't know what they want.

If you are not achieving the wealth you desire, there's a good chance it's because, first, you subconsciously don't really want wealth, or second, you're not willing to do what it takes to create it.

Three Levels of Wanting

Below insightful excerpt from the book 'Secrets of the Millionaire Mind' by T. Harv Eker on three levels of so-called wanting.

First Level

The first level is "I want to be rich." That's another way of saying, "I'll take it if it falls in my lap." Wanting alone is useless. Have you noticed that wanting doesn't necessarily lead to "having"? Notice also that wanting without having led to more wanting. Wanting becomes habitual and leads only to itself, creating a perfect circle that goes exactly nowhere. Wealth does not come from merely wanting it.

How do you know this is true? With a simple reality check: billions of people want to be rich, but relatively few are.

Second Level

The second level of wanting is "I choose to be rich." This entails deciding to become rich. Choosing is a much stronger energy and goes hand in hand with being responsible for creating your reality. The word decision comes from the Latin word decidere, which means "to kill off any other alternatives." Choosing is better but not best.

Third Level (Most Important!)

The third level of wanting is "I commit to being rich." The definition of the word commit is "to devote oneself unreservedly." This means holding absolutely nothing back; giving 100 percent of everything you've got to achieve wealth. It means being willing to do whatever it takes for as long as it takes. This is the warrior's way. No excuses, no ifs, no buts, no maybes—and failure is not an option. The warrior's way is simple: "I will be rich or I will die trying."

"I commit to being rich." Try saying that to yourself....What comes up for you? For some, it feels empowering. For others, it feels daunting.

Most people would never truly commit to being rich. If you asked them, "Would you bet your life that in the next ten years, you will be wealthy?" most would say, "No way!" That's the difference between rich people and poor people. It's precise because people won't truly commit to being rich that they are not rich and most likely never will be.

Some might say, "What are you talking about? I work my butt off, I'm trying really hard. Of course, I'm committed to being rich." And I would reply, "That you're trying means little. The definition of commitment is to devote oneself unreservedly." The key word is unreserved. Which means you're putting everything, and I mean everything, you've got into it. Most people I know who are not financially successful have limits on how much they are willing to do, how much they are willing to risk, and how much they are willing to sacrifice. Although they think they're willing to do whatever it takes, upon deeper questioning I always find they have plenty of conditions around what they are willing to do and not do to succeed!

Way Ahead to Getting Rich

Getting rich is not a stroll in the park, It takes focus, courage, knowledge, expertise, 100 percent of your effort, a never-give-up attitude, and of course a rich mindset. You also have to believe in your heart of hearts that you can create wealth and that you absolutely deserve it. Again, what this means is that, if you are not fully, totally, and truly committed to creating wealth, chances are you won't.

Rich people are totally clear that they want wealth. They are steady in their desire. They are fully committed to creating wealth. As long as it's legal, moral, and ethical, they will do whatever it takes to have wealth. Rich people do not send mixed messages to the universe. Poor people do.

Are you willing to work sixteen hours a day? Rich people are. Are you willing to work seven days a week and give up most of your weekends? Rich people are. Are you willing to sacrifice seeing your family, your friends, and give up your recreation and hobbies? Rich people are. Are you willing to risk all your time, energy, and start-up capital with no guarantee of returns? Rich people are.

For a time, hopefully, a short time but often a long time, rich people are ready and willing to do all of the above. Are you?

It's interesting to note, however, that once you do commit, the universe will bend over backward to support you and even create miracles for you. But first, you have to commit!

"Resenting the rich is one of the surest ways to stay broke"— T. Harv Eker

*****

19. How to Achieve a Wealthy Life! Getting Rich Begins with Your Thinking

Most people want to live a wealthy life in the world. But only a few achieve that. Why is it so? If we divide this world financially, there will be three groups *Rich, Middle class and Poor*. Each group manage their financial legacy generation after generation. Out of these three groups, the middle class fights the battle to come in a rich group. But once they feel that their financial life has improved, the richness scale changes.

Middle-class people believe in hard work and have linear thinking about money. From childhood, so many negative beliefs are set in their mind about money, which keeps on impacting them even in their adulthood. These limiting beliefs work as a hindrance in their journey towards richness. Thinking of these groups about money & wealthy people is completely the opposite of thinking of rich people.

This astonished thinking has been compared by Steve Siebold in his book titled "How Rich People Think". This book is a result of his more than 20 years of research on this topic & gives a grateful insight into the thinking of rich people and middle-class people.

Money to Retire or to Impact the World

When Steve Siebold began studying the ultra-successful and super-rich in 1984, he thought they were more ambitious than the average person. Later he discovered after hundreds of interviews that it wasn't the lack of desire that held the masses back from getting wealthy, but the lack of belief in their own ability to make it happen.

The average person is carrying around so many limiting beliefs about money it's a miracle they acquire any at all. Without some intervention, a lucky break, or exposure to a book or series of blogs on these topics, most people have little or no chance of ever becoming rich. The sad thing is, they have everything they need to make more money than they can spend, and without the interference of a slew of middle-class beliefs, they would accomplish it.

The problem is outside the consciousness-expanding world of personal development, the masses are never taught the power beliefs have on our behaviours and results. Beliefs literally control everything we do unless they are interrupted consciously through free will or upgraded through programming. Their fear and scarcity-based thinking lead them to look at everything through the filters of scepticism and cynicism as a protective mechanism.

With this limited thinking, the masses major goal with money is to retire at 65 and hopefully have enough money to survive until they die.

The world-class, while often no more ambitious, set their sights on impacting the world with their wealth. Some do it through philanthropy, others through business or various financial vehicles. They do all of this while living the good life materially and enjoying the peace of mind that comes along with being rich.

Role of Intelligence in Richness!

The masses see the rich as a special segment of society that views themselves as better than everyone else. This myth is perpetuated by people who are disappointed in their own lack of success and envious of those who have made it big.

The truth is, wealthy people don't think they are smarter or better, and they admire people who have the courage and endurance to labour all their lives for meagre compensation. It's hard not to admire the coal miner or bricklayer who slogs to work every day for forty years and barely lives a frugal life. Hard labour jobs are a poor strategy for acquiring money, but they do garner respect.

Self-made millionaires know getting rich has little to do with intelligence and everything to do with focus and persistence. They know the average person is more focused on playing video games, surfing the internet and watching television than he or she is on building a portfolio. That's why many millionaires are high school and college dropouts. They quit school because they didn't see the purpose of what they were learning.

Many school curriculums are too broad in scope, outdated and lack the proper data to teach what it takes to be successful. Most teachers have no idea how to build a fortune. While wealthy people believe in formal education, few credit their financial empires to what they learned in school.

Getting rich is not about being smarter, more educated or intelligent: it's about knowing what you want and being laser-focused on getting it no matter how long it takes or how hard you have to work. It's simple, but not easy.

Dependence or Self-Reliance Thinking

Since the masses believe people become wealthy through luck, good fortune or social advantage, they think it's only fair that the rich disperse their money to those who have less. This socialistic philosophy is rooted in the belief that everyone is his *brother's keeper*.

The world class believes every citizen in a free market economy has the opportunity to become wealthy. They believe getting rich is a choice. While wealthy people have the most to give and are the most charitable people on the planet, they give for the sake of giving and not from any moral code or societal pressure.

They believe giving people unearned rewards robs them of the satisfaction they will experience from their own achievements. The world class believe in self-reliance as a guiding principle in their lives, but at the same time, they realize the tendency of the middle class to fall into a victim mentality that expects someone else to take care of them.

Through fear and scarcity-based thinking, this seems not only fair but the most socially evolved method of government. Through the eyes of love and abundance, this type of funding is the surest way to psychologically paralyze the population into believing that they can't take care of themselves and have no hope of ever accomplishing anything on their own.

Getting Rich Begins With Your Thinking

The masses do not understand the nature of building wealth, which is why generation after generation approaches it the same way and almost always fails.

Schools teach the basics of balancing a chequebook, adhering to a budget, and basic math. This trains children and young adults to think about money in linear, logical terms which can seal their fate financially before they earn their high school diploma.

The fact is: getting rich begins with the way you think and what you believe about making money. If your parents were broke or in the middle class, you will end up the same if you adopt their beliefs and philosophies about money. Critical thinking says the only reason people settle for a mediocre, middle-class existence is that they are unaware of how to move beyond it.

The secret has always been the same: thinking. The only way to learn how to think like a rich person is to study them. While the masses believe becoming wealthy is out of their control, the world class knows earning money and amassing wealth is a cause-and-effect relationship. The cause of our behaviour is our belief system, and the effect of our behaviour is the result we get. Change the cause, and by default, you automatically change the behaviour and bottom-line result. Knowing this, the world-class thinker is always upgrading her beliefs and philosophies on money by studying those who are wealthier.

"Wealth is power. With wealth many things are possible."
- George Clason

*****

20. Secrets of Billionaires - What it takes to move from millionaire to billionaire?

Secrets of billionaires have been revealed from time to time by carrying out years of interactive research work on them. In 1908, when Napoleon Hill was assigned an interview with Andrew Carnegie—the wealthiest man in the world at the time—he didn't imagine the journey that was awaiting him. Carnegie, himself an extremely successful entrepreneur, had the conviction that something resembling a success formula must exist—one that could be shaped into a reliable system that anybody could follow.

Impressed by Hill's intellect, Carnegie asked him if he was up to the task of formulating such a system by interviewing the most successful people in America and analyzing the results. Hill grab that opportunity. Carnegie gave him a letter of introduction to automotive magnate Henry Ford. The latter then introduced him to Alexander Graham Bell (inventor of the telephone), Elmer R. Gates (inventor of the fire extinguisher), Thomas Edison (inventor of the light bulb), and Luther Burbank (agricultural pioneer).

Hill went on to interview these individuals and many others who were among the wealthiest and most successful people of his time. After 20 years of research, he published his Philosophy of Achievement as a formula for rags-to-riches success in his monumental work *The Law of Success*. He condensed this knowledge into his famous work *Think and Grow Rich,* which went on to become one of the best-selling books of all time—and continues to sell in multiple versions and formats.

Billionaire's Secret

A similar task has been done by Rafael Badziag to make us understand billionaire's life and their success secrets. He had done interviews with more than twenty self-made billionaires across the globe. Most of them are not from developed countries and also not having strong family backgrounds.

Have you ever asked yourself why is it that despite all your hustle every day, you aren't where you want to be in life? How is it possible that some people during one life span manage to build organizations of hundreds of thousands of people and create the amount of value that an average person would need hundreds of thousands of years to create? What is their secret? Is it just a question of lucky circumstances? Is it their environment? Maybe it is their education? Or does the secret lie in their personalities? What are the keys to their phenomenal success? What do their belief systems consist of? And what are the mindsets and success rituals that these influential people have used to create such massive wealth? What drives them? What is the source of their exceptional motivation? And what gives them the energy to relentlessly pursue such outrageous goals? What is it in the personalities of self-made billionaires that made them achieve so much more than an average entrepreneur and become so extremely successful in business?

The book 'The Billion Dollar Secret' is the result of a five-year journey that took Rafael Badziag, several times around the globe to find the answers to these questions. Some of the excerpts from this outstanding work-

Limitless Desire for Growth

The scale of your thinking determines the size of your achievements, so you better be ambitious and dream big. In order to become BIG, you need to think BIG and have a limitless desire for growth.

Manny Stul, the World Entrepreneur of the Year 2016, has built two companies in his career. With the first, a gift distributor, he became a millionaire, with the second, a toy manufacturer—a billionaire. "I think desire is very, very important. If you desire to be a million dollars or you desire to be a billion dollars, very big difference. There's a different scale and different scope about which you operate. I certainly had no desire to be a billionaire; I just wanted to be extremely successful. I'd say the difference is desire, scale, and vision. Thinking on a larger scale, thinking on a bigger scale. When I started my gift company, I could've just wanted to be successful in Perth, but I always wanted to be successful in Australia. With Moose, my second company, I didn't want to be successful in Australia, I wanted to be successful worldwide. They're just different scales of thinking."

What Is a Billionaire?

A billionaire is a person with a net worth of at least $1 billion (> ₹ 7,000 Crore). Let us understand this figure-

- If a person is earning a net of ₹ 50 Lakhs/year, then it will take more than *14,000* years to have $1 billion
- If a person is earning a net of ₹ 5 Crore/year, then it will take more than *1,400* years to have $1 billion

Being a billionaire is an extraordinary achievement and it requires an extraordinary thought process. What you may not realize is that a billionaire is an extremely scarce creature. Statistically, only 1 out of every 5 million citizens in the world—or 1 in 10,000 millionaires—is a billionaire.

Seldom do these people have billions of dollars sitting in their personal bank accounts, either; when they do, this is only for a limited time between transactions. Rather, almost all of their money is invested in companies, stock, and/or real estate. It would be irresponsible to have so much cash lying around. The money would be eaten up by inflation, and there is also always the risk of a bank going bankrupt.

Artist Michael Marcovici created a work of art, One Billion Dollar, which physically depicted $1 billion in printed money. When the piece was exhibited in Vienna, Austria, Marcovici was asked why he didn't use real money. His answer? Nobody could afford the ticket. Even if he borrowed it at only 1% a year interest from a bank, it would cost around $200,000 to have that real money used in a one-week exposition.

An entrepreneur or investor usually wants to see profit from his money—say 5%. In this case, keeping $1 billion in cash around the house would mean $135,000 opportunity cost each and every day. This is more than most people earn in a year. Few people do this voluntarily.

Difference Between Billionaire & Millionaire

Many people fail to see the difference between a millionaire and a billionaire. In reality, the differences are gigantic. Consider the following examples for reference-

- An average millionaire may own a hotel. Norwegian billionaire Petter Stordalen owns a chain of almost 200 hotels.

- A wealthy multimillionaire may own a factory. Canadian billionaire Frank Stronach owns 400 of them.
- A millionaire may own a restaurant or possibly even several. Jack Cowin, an Australian billionaire, has interests in 3,000 restaurants.
- The run-of-the-mill millionaire may own a supermarket or two. Russian billionaire Sergey Galitskiy owns over 17,000 supermarkets and drugstores.

The gap between millionaires and billionaires is colossal not only with respect to their wealth but also in terms of the power and impact they have. Billionaires literally change the world.

Billionaire's Vision

Cai Dongqing, called the Chinese Walt Disney, stresses that you need to dare to dream and fight for it. Asked about the difference between millionaires and billionaires, he says: "They have different goals which will decide whether they will get going or feel satisfied with the status quo after they have reached the first level of success."

That's also what Frank Stronach, the Canadian billionaire and founder of Magna, confirms: "Once you stop dreaming, you're a dead person. There's no limit to dreaming. It's unlimited. Knowledge is limited. You must always have dreams. Once you have a dream, then you daydream, and then you say what you have to do to maybe fulfill those dreams."

Dreaming big is one thing. Doing big things is another. Michał Sołowow, the wealthiest person in Poland, shares an interesting perspective on this: "I went into construction because I have always believed that by making things big and expensive, I will obtain much greater margins than by doing small and cheap things. Therefore, instead of producing a hand-cleaning paste for a dollar, I preferred to build a building for $10 million. Assuming that by producing a hand-cleaning paste the margin will be none or minimal. In my construction industry, the money was big, and in consequence, I had more of it at my disposal and managed to use it."

So break up the limits that hold you back and do a bigger thing!

"If you don't find a way to make money while you sleep, you will work until you die." - <u>Warren Buffett</u>

*****

21. How to Protect & Invest Wealth? Just follow these five golden rules!

Creating wealth is one skill, but to protect & invest wealth is altogether a different set of skills. It is much more difficult to protect wealth compare to creating it. We have seen so many peoples around us, who had earned so much money in their lifetime but left with no money at a later phase of their life.

The key principle of 'how to protect and invest wealth' has been listed in one of my all-time favorite books 'The Richest Man in Babylon' by George S. Clason. Before proceeding to these principles/laws, let us understand the interesting background of Babylon's development.

History of Babylon

In the pages of history, there lives no city more glamorous than Babylon. Its very name conjures visions of wealth and splendor. Its treasures of gold and jewels were fabulous. One naturally pictures such a wealthy city as located in a suitable setting of tropical luxury, surrounded by rich natural resources of forests and mines. *Such was not the case.* It was located beside the Euphrates River, in a flat, arid valley. It had no forests, no mines—not even stone for building. Also, it was not even located upon a natural trade route. The rainfall was insufficient to raise crops.

Man-Developed Civilization

Babylon is an outstanding example of man's ability to achieve great objectives, using whatever means are at his disposal. All of the resources supporting this large city were man-developed. All of its riches were man-made.

Babylon possessed just two natural resources—fertile soil and water in the river. With one of the greatest engineering accomplishments of this or any other day, Babylonian engineers diverted the waters from the river by means of dams and immense irrigation canals. Far out across that arid valley went these canals to pour the life-giving waters over the fertile soil. This ranks among the first engineering feats known to history. Such abundant crops were the reward of this irrigation system the world had never seen before.

As a city, Babylon exists no more. When those energizing human forces that built and maintained the city for thousands of years were withdrawn, it soon became a deserted ruin. The site of the city is in Asia about six hundred miles east of the Suez Canal, just north of the Persian Gulf. The latitude is about thirty degrees above the Equator, practically the same as that of Yuma, Arizona. It possessed a climate similar to that of this American city, hot and dry.

Many scientists consider the civilization of Babylon and other cities in this valley to be the oldest of which there is a definite record. Positive dates have been proved to reach *back 8000 years*.

Preservation of Wisdom

Ancient math book? The Babylonians wrote sophisticated mathematical procedures in cuneiform script on clay tablets MATHIEU OSSENDRIJVER, SCIENCE/AAAS

The glory of Babylon has faded but its wisdom has been preserved for us. For this, we are indebted to their form of records. In that distant day, the use of paper had not been invented. Instead, they laboriously engraved their writing upon tablets of moist clay. When completed, these were baked and became hard tile. In size, they were about six by eight inches and an inch in thickness.

These clay tablets, as they are commonly called, were used much as we use modern forms of writing. Upon them were engraved legends, poetry, history, transcriptions of royal decrees, the laws of the land, titles to property, promissory notes, and even letters that were dispatched by messengers to distant cities. From these clay tablets, we are permitted an insight into the intimate, personal affairs of the people. For example, one tablet, evidently from the records of a country storekeeper, relates that upon the given date a certain named customer brought in a cow and exchanged it for seven sacks of wheat, three being delivered at the time and the other four to await the customer's pleasure.

Five Laws of Gold

The Richest Man in Babylon hand out financial advice through a collection of parables set 4,000 years ago in ancient Babylon. This book remains in print almost a century after the parables were originally published, and is regarded as a classic of personal financial advice.

The parables are told by a fictional Babylonian character called Arkad, a poor scribe who became the "richest man in

Babylon". Arkad shared his advice on 'how to generate money and wealth' & 'how to protect and invest wealth' to the people of Babylon. All these pieces of advice are eternal advice and hold true at any given point in time.

'How to protect and Invest wealth' advice is compiled in the form of 'Five Laws of Gold'. The meaning of Gold here in the current scenario is Money, Wealth.

<u>The First Law of Gold</u>

Gold cometh gladly and in increasing quantity to any man who will put by not less than one-tenth of his earnings to create an estate for his future and that of his family.

"Any man who will put by one-tenth of his earnings consistently and invest it wisely will surely create a valuable estate that will provide an income for him in the future and further guarantee safety for his family in case the gods call him to the world of darkness. This law always says that gold comes gladly to such a man. I can truly certify this in my own life. The more gold I accumulate, the more readily it comes to me and in increased quantities. The gold which I save earns more, even as yours will, and its earnings earn more, and this is the working out of the first law."

<u>The Second Law of Gold</u>

Gold laboreth diligently and contentedly for the wise owner who finds for it profitable employment, multiplying even as the flocks of the field.

"Gold, indeed, is a willing worker. It is ever eager to multiply when the opportunity presents itself. To every man who has a store of gold set by, opportunity comes for its most profitable use. As the years' pass, it multiplies itself in surprising fashion."

The Third Law of Gold

Gold clingeth to the protection of the cautious owner who invests it under the advice of men wise in its handling.

"Gold, indeed, adhere to the cautious owner, even as it flees the careless owner. The man who seeks the advice of men wise in handling gold soon learn not to jeopardize his treasure, but to preserve in safety and to enjoy in contentment its consistent increase."

The Fourth Law of Gold

Gold slippeth away from the man who invests it in businesses or purposes with which he is not familiar or which are not approved by those skilled in its keep.

"To the man who has gold, yet is not skilled in its handling, many uses for it appear most profitable. Too often these are fraught with the danger of loss, and if properly analyzed by wise men, show a small possibility of profit. Therefore, the inexperienced owner of gold who trusts to his own judgment and invests it in business or purposes with which he is not familiar, too often finds his judgment imperfect and pays with his treasure for his inexperience. Wise, indeed is he who invests his treasures under the advice of men skilled in the ways of gold."

The Fifth Law of Gold

Gold flees the man who would force it to impossible earnings or who followeth the alluring advice of tricksters and schemers or who trusts it to his own inexperience and romantic desires in investment.

"Curious propositions that thrill like adventure tales always come to the new owner of gold. These appear to grant his treasure with magic powers that will enable it to make impossible earnings. Yet attentiveness the wise men for verily they know the risks that lurk behind every plan to make great wealth suddenly."

They are not secrets but truths which every man must first learn and then follow who wishes to step out to improve his or her financial life.

"You must gain control over your money or the lack of it will forever control you." - Dave Ramsey

*****

22. Focus on Opportunities or Obstacles ! What you focus on expands...

Which one to focus on, Opportunities or Obstacles? Almost all people will say that obviously on opportunities. But do we really focus on them? Most of the time, most people focus on possible obstacles during their financial journey in life.

Whatever you focus on, it expands. What is the focus area of rich people, its opportunities? And what is the focus for poor people, its obstacles. Rich people see potential growth. Poor people see potential loss. Rich people focus on the rewards. Poor focus on the risks.

I shall redirect this point to psychology. Our subconscious mind feeds us what we ask for each and every time. It doesn't understand whether one particular word has a positive or negative meaning. It simply focuses on that word and keeps on feeding you similar or related experiences.

Some psychologists believe that the subconscious mind does not see the "not.". Though you do not want obstacles in your financial life, if you focus on them even to avoid them, you will still get obstacles. So we must change our focus from obstacles to opportunities.

Role of the Subconscious Mind

It comes down to the age-old question, "Is the glass half empty or half full?" We're not talking about positive thinking here, we're talking about your habitual perspective on the world. Poor people make choices based on fear. Their minds are constantly scanning for what is wrong or could go wrong in any situation. Their primary mindset is "What if it doesn't work?" or, more often, "It won't work."

Here again, fear is one of the strong emotions and totally influences our subconscious mind. Our conscious mind or intelligence says that we will succeed but at the same time, we have fear of failure in one corner of our mind. In such situations, fear of failure always wins over the desire for success. And this happens because more than 90 % of our life is controlled by our subconscious mind day to day & fear has a direct connection with our subconscious mind, so it wins.

We need to harmonize the conscious and subconscious minds together to become financially successful. If these two are not working together, there is a very rare chance that you will get a high level of success.

Middle-class people are slightly more optimistic. Their mindset is "I sure hope this works."

Take Responsibility for Results

Rich people, as we've said earlier, take responsibility for the results in their lives and act upon the mindset "It will work because I'll make it work." Rich people expect to succeed. They have confidence in their abilities & creativity. If one way is not working, they find another way to succeed.

Generally speaking, the higher the reward, the higher the risk. Because they constantly see opportunities, rich people are willing to take a risk. Rich people believe that, if worse comes to worst, they can always make their money back.

Poor people, on the other hand, expect to fail. They lack confidence in themselves and in their abilities. Poor people believe that if things do not move in the desired direction, it would be catastrophic. And because they constantly see obstacles, they are usually unwilling to take a risk. No risk, no reward.

For the record, being willing to risks doesn't necessarily mean that you are willing to lose. Rich people take educated risks. This means that they do research, do their due diligence, and make decisions based on solid information and facts. Do rich people take forever to get educated? No. They do what they can in as short a time as possible, then make an informed decision to go for it or not.

<u>Getting Ready…But Always?</u>

Although poor people claim to be preparing for opportunities, what they're usually doing is stalling. They're scared to death, hemming, and hawing for weeks, months, and even years on end, and by then the opportunity usually disappears. Then they rationalize the situation by saying, "I was getting ready." Sure enough, but while they were "getting ready," the rich guy got in, got out, and made another fortune.

In business, how many times have you heard of a guy who plops some money down on a piece of land in the boonies (*where nobody lives*), and ten years later, some conglomerate decides it wants to build a shopping center or office building on it? This investor gets rich. So, was it a brilliant business move on his part or sheer luck? My guess is that it's a bit of both.

The point, however, is that no luck—or anything else worthwhile—will come your way unless you take some form of action. To succeed financially, you have to do something, buy something, or start something. And when you do, is it luck, or is it the universe or a higher power supporting you in its miraculous ways for having the courage and commitment to go for it? As far as I'm concerned, who cares what it is. It happens!

Focus Area Leads Life

Your field of focus determines what you find in life. Focus on opportunities and that's what you find. Focus on obstacles and that's what you find. I'm not saying that you don't take care of problems. Of course, handle problems as they arise, in the present. But keep your eye on your goal, and keep moving toward your target. Put your time and energy into creating what you want. When obstacles arise, see yourself as bigger than any obstacle and handle them, then quickly refocus on your vision. You do not make your life about solving problems. You don't spend all your time-fighting fires. Those who do, move backward! You spend your time and energy in thought and deed, moving steadily forward, toward your goal.

Do you want some simple but extremely rare advice? Here it is: If you want to get rich, focus on making, keeping, and investing your money. If you want to be poor, focus on spending your money. You can read a thousand books and take a hundred courses on success, but it all boils down to that. Remember, what you focus on expands.

Wait for 100 % Information?

Rich people also understand that you can never know all the information beforehand. Get ready the best you can in as short a time as possible; take action; then correct along the way.

It's nuts to think you can know everything that may happen in the future. It's delusional to believe you can prepare for every circumstance that might someday occur and protect yourself from it. Did you know that there are no straight lines in the universe? Life doesn't travel in perfectly straight lines. It moves more like a winding river. More often than not, you can only see to the next bend, and only when you reach that next turn can you see more.

<u>Better to Act Now</u>

To harness opportunities, we need to take action. Action always beats inaction. Rich people get started. They trust that once they get in the game, they can make intelligent decisions in the present moment, make corrections, and adjust their sails along the way.

Poor people don't trust in themselves or their abilities, so they believe they have to know everything in advance, which is virtually impossible. In the end, by telling themselves, "I'm not doing anything until I've identified every possible problem and know exactly what to do about it," poor people never take action and therefore always lose. Rich people see an opportunity, jump on it, and get even richer. As for poor people? They're still "preparing"! *(content source inspired from '<u>Secrets of the Millionaire Mind</u>' by <u>T. Harv Eker)</u>*

"Wealth flows from energy and ideas."- ***<u>William Feather</u>***

*****

23. Choice ! (Being Rich or Poor) - Alter the trajectory of your future!

Choice plays a very important role at different phases of life to set our destiny. It depends on us whether we need to improve our financial life or continue the current struggling life.

(Now search your favorite blogs related to Mind, Money & Business by typing the keyword in search icon available at top of page @ www.fastlanefreedom.com)

Symptom or Cause?

If poorness were an illness, take a guess as to its cause. Of course, lack of money. But is that a cause or a symptom of the underlying problem? Lack of education? Lack of opportunity, positive role models, or determination? Those are all symptoms. If you retrace poverty's footprints you will find that poorness starts at the exact same place: choice. The leading cause of poorness is poor choices.

If your car's fuel tank had a small leak, how would you fix it? The symptomatic solver would increase his trips to the gas station to ensure a steady inflow of fuel. The problematic solver plugs up the hole. One addresses the symptom (the gas tank leaks), while the other addresses the problem (there's a hole in the gas tank). While adding fuel addresses the symptom, it doesn't solve the problem.

How does this relate to success and choices?

Simple: If you aren't where you want to be, the problem is your choices.

It's Not About One Choice

Your circumstances are the symptoms of those choices. For example, everyone loves success quotes. Here are two:

'The will to persevere is often the difference between failure and success.'

'Success means having the courage, the determination, and the will to become the person you believe you were meant to be.'

The problem with these quotes is they're ambiguous to the real issue.

The first quote deals with perseverance. How do you persevere? You react from conscious choice. Not just one choice but hundreds, perhaps thousands. You cannot choose to persevere with one choice. You cannot wake up one day and say, "Oh, today I will choose to persevere." It must happen every day, not just once! Perseverance is woven by many choices that fabricate lifestyle. If you quit after two tries, have you persevered? Can you claim perseverance after one failure?

Likewise, the second quote suffers from the same problem. Determination is not a solitary choice but thousands of them. You cannot decide to be determined; it must occur repeatedly and with commitment.

It isn't one choice but hundreds. And when you line a string of choices together, they create your process, and your process will create your lifestyle. Lifestyle choices will make you a millionaire.

Choice and You

There's a big chasm between thinking wealth and choosing wealth. You can choose to align your life with greater purpose or choose to let life live you. You can choose to believe these theories or choose not to. The common denominator is CHOICE and YOU.

Your steering wheel (choice) is the most powerful control you have in your life. People don't choose to be poor. They make poor decisions that slowly assemble into a poorness puzzle. Retrace the footprints to poverty and it happens slowly, systematically, and methodically, under a steady diet of poor choices.

- The choice to cheat on your exams or study.
- The choice to lie or to be honest.
- The choice to drive without insurance.
- The choice to befriend bad people over good people.
- The choice to watch TV or read a book.
- The choice to drive 105 mph in a 55 mph zone.
- The choice to overindulge in food or liquor.
- The choice to believe in people with no track record.
- The choice to buy on credit.
- The choice to hire a contractor without a background check.
- The choice to play video games 30 hours a week.
- The choice to go into business with incompetent partners.

A Fastlane millionaire by age 28, Andre has everything: money, a beautiful wife, a healthy baby, and seven restaurants scattered across the Five Boroughs. Andre is on top of the world and feels invincible. One Friday night after a few drinks to celebrate his night manager's birthday, Andre drives home sloppy drunk. He chooses to think, "I'm OK." On his way home he gets into an accident and kills a family of four. Andre is arrested for drunk driving and charged with manslaughter. After his conviction, he spends the next 11 years of his life in prison. He loses his business and his family.

Andre's life forever changed because of multiple treasonous choices. The choice to drink. The choice to drive. The choice to think, "I'm OK." The series of choices are plentiful, his exit strategy is clear. He doesn't choose wisely.

Your life's steering wheel is a dangerous weapon. Three inches is all it takes. Jerk your life's wheel three tiny inches while speeding and you can steer your life onto a path of no return, or worse, smack into a concrete wall. Like an automobile's steering wheel, your choices are super-sensitive. Unfortunately, treasonous roads always have a green light. People drown in the misery of their own choices while neglecting to acknowledge they are the cause.

The Butterfly Effect

Can you make a choice this instant that can forever alter the trajectory of your future? You can, and it can be the difference between poverty and wealth.

When you make minor permutations (choices) that deviate from your initial conditions, profound effects transpire over time.

Think of it like a golf club striking a golf ball.

When the clubface hits the ball square, the ball goes straight and heads toward the hole. But when the clubface has rotated a fraction of one degree, the ball's trajectory lands far off course. At impact, the divergence is minor, but as the ball travels further it widens and widens until the gap is so large that getting back on track is nearly impossible. A bad choice can set your trajectory off by only one degree today, but over years the error is magnified.

Choices have this type of divergence over time and it's called "impact differential." When your choices are extrapolated throughout the years, the divergence widens. The divergence can be either positive or negative.

Recognize that every day you make decisions that will ripple through the years. Question is, will your choice ripple to happiness and wealth? Or depression and poverty?

Way Ahead

So make a better choice to improve your financial life. Once you decide to improve with deep faith, your mind is there to guide you, just listen to it. But be sure that you are not having contradictory thoughts about money, otherwise, you will be at the same place, where you are right now.

When your health is not well, then what do you do? You simply visit a doctor (expert), take medicine, and then get fit.

But when your financial condition is not well, then what do you do? Many a time not much? Even you avoid discussion on this topic among others and you keep on struggling. You think that you are the expert in managing money, but you are not.

Earning money & managing it well is also a skill and each skill can be mastered by increasing the domain knowledge of that.

e.g. if your investments are not giving good returns, go into the detail, find out the cause & then take actions to improve the situation. If you go into the detail, definitely you will find the causes to correct and then make a better choice. Being rich a right!

(Excerpts are inspired from one of my favorite books, *The Millionaire Fastlane* by *MJ DeMarco*)

"Rich people have small TVs and big libraries, and poor people have small libraries and big TVs." – *Zig Ziglar*

*****

24. Billionaires Who Born Poor! One of them is worth more than $ 80 billion...

More than 70 % of billionaires are self-made billionaires across the world and this has been proven time and again by various financial surveys like Forbes' Billionaire List-2021 or Rich List 2020 (IIFL Wealth Hurun India). Many of the world's richest people came from humble backgrounds to become billionaires, with childhood poverty, war, and other issues driving them on to succeed.

Here are some of the wealthiest people on the planet who survived a challenging upbringing and went on to build huge billion-dollar empires. *($ 1 billion is a huge amount to earn in a lifetime, it is > ₹ 7300 Crore as of May 2021)*

(Now search your favorite blogs related to Mind, Money & Business by typing the keyword in search icon available at top of page)

Kenny Troutt

Now worth $1.5 billion

Telecommunications genius and self-made billionaire Kenny Troutt has now retired but not before making a cool $1.5 billion fortune. An avid horse racing fan, Troutt owns WinStar Farm in Kentucky and is a breeder of Thoroughbreds. Troutt's fortune also allowed him to sponsor his son's nationally competitive basketball team for years and even provide them rides to tournaments on his private jet.

Journey Snaps

The son of a single mother who worked as a bartender, Troutt grew up in public housing in Mount Vernon, Illinois. What he lacked in funds he made up for in determination, paying his way through Southern Illinois University by selling insurance alongside studying.

In 1988 Kenny Troutt founded long-distance phone company Excel Communications and in 1996 Troutt took the company public. In 1998, Troutt sold Excel Communications to Teleglobe in a $3.5 billion deal and reinvested the profits in stocks, bonds, and horses.

David Murdock

Now worth $2.1 billion

David Murdock, worth $2.1 billion, is the chairman of privately-held Dole Food Products and Castle & Cooke. He owns residential and commercial properties in Arizona, California, and Hawaii and a collection of Arabian horses. The 95-year-old has also donated heavily to longevity research and vows to live until he is 125.

Journey Snaps

Murdock, who is dyslexic, dropped out of high school in the ninth grade and worked at a gas station before being drafted into the Army in 1943. After serving in World War II, Murdock found himself homeless with little more than a dollar to his name.

After borrowing $900 from a good Samaritan he bought a diner in Detroit and flipped it for a tidy profit. He used the proceeds to buy a car, drive to Arizona, and started Castle & Cooke, a real estate company that grew to include Dole Foods Co, a fresh fruit and vegetable producer.

Mohed Altrad

Now worth $3.5 billion

EY World Entrepreneur of the Year 2015 and Montpellier rugby club president Mohed Altrad is worth $3.5 billion. He heads up the Altrad Group, which provides construction and maintenance services, but his start in life was worlds apart from this. Of his past he said: "I had no special dream - only the ambition not to accept my initial destiny."

Journey Snaps

Mohed Altrad came from humble beginnings, born an orphaned Bedouin in the Syrian desert. Raised by his grandmother, Altrad was banned from going to school, but an innate drive to learn saw him attending school anyway. He eventually won a scholarship to study in France despite speaking no French and having very little money.

In France, Altrad was poor and lived off one meal a day, yet managed to earn himself an undergraduate degree in physics and math, and a Ph.D. in computer science. In 1985, after a short spell working for a tech firm and the Abu Dhabi National Oil Company, Altrad bought a bankrupt scaffolding manufacturer in France. With his partner, he created the world's leading scaffolding company.

To find more about his journey, you can read the blog 'No Well Off, Still a Self-Made Billionaire'

Oprah Winfrey

Now worth $2.6 billion

Media Mogul Oprah Winfrey, worth $2.6 billion, is an American media executive, talk show host, actress, producer, and philanthropist. She has a large number of A-lister friends and an impressive number of mansions. Her 65-acre Californian estate is large enough for Winfrey to run a two-mile route without leaving the property.

Journey Snaps

Winfrey overcame a tough childhood, born to a teen mother in rural Mississippi and raised without indoor plumbing. She was determined to break away, earning herself a scholarship to Tennessee State University and becoming the first African American TV correspondent in the state at just 19. Winfrey then parlayed her role as a news anchor into a 25-year talk show gig.

Winfrey's hit talk show has transitioned into a media and business empire, including a magazine and cable channel, OWN. Her 25.5% of the network is worth about $75 million and Winfrey also owns an 8% stake in Weight Watchers, acting as their brand ambassador. Reinvested, the profits from her show add up to nearly $2 billion.

Zhang Xin

Now worth $3.1 billion

Chinese billionaire businesswoman Zhang Xin has an estimated worth of $3.1 billion and has been called the 'woman who built Beijing' due to her groundbreaking career in property. But nothing was handed to Xin on a plate.

Journey Snaps

Born in Beijing in 1965, during the Cultural Revolution, Xin grew up with her mother after her parents divorced when she was five. Mother and daughter moved to Hong Kong when Xin was 14 and, to make ends meet, they both got jobs as factory workers. Xin was determined to learn however and would attend evening school after work. Aged 19, Xin flew to England to learn English at a language school in Oxford. She got a job at a fish and chip shop to stay afloat.

Xin went on to study at both Sussex and Cambridge universities before landing a job at Goldman Sachs, where she worked in floating Chinese factories on the public stock exchange. In 1995, Xin and her husband founded property development company SOHO China. To date, the company has developed over 60 million square feet of land.

Jan Koum

Now worth $10.3 billion

Instant messaging whizz Jan Koum is worth $10.3 billion. In April 2018, Koum announced his impending departure from Facebook HQ in California. However he continues to work one day a month and banks close to half a billion dollars every financial quarter, stalling until his remaining stock options vest.

Journey Snaps

When Jan Koum moved to California from Ukraine as a teen his family struggled to stay above the poverty line. Koum relied on food stamps and swept floors to make ends meet. Despite his tough upbringing, Koum worked hard at school. By the age of 18 Koum became interested in programming and enrolled at San Jose State University.

In 1997, Koum was hired by Yahoo! as an infrastructure engineer where he worked for nearly nine years before leaving aged 30 with enough cash to launch his own business. In 2009 Koum co-founded the real-time messaging app WhatsApp. The app was so successful Facebook bought it for a massive $19 billion and Koum was invited to sit on the Facebook board.

Amancio Ortega

Now worth $82.1 billion

Amancio Ortega has a mammoth net worth of $82.1 billion and is one of the wealthiest person in the world. How did he do it? He co-founded Inditex, best known for its Zara fashion chain. Ortega started Zara in 1975 and saw it grow to 2,208 stores in 96 countries by 2020. But Ortega came from very humble beginnings.

Journey Snaps

Ortega was born in 1936, just before the outbreak of Spain's Civil War, and grew up in Leon where his father was a railway worker. Artega left school at 14, moved to A Coruña, and started working as a shop hand at a local shirt maker. This is where he learnt to make clothes by hand.

Once Ortega had gained enough experience, he and his wife launched a textile manufacturing company then, later on, the Zara brand. Zara soon became very successful due to its quick turnaround of stock and stores opened all around the globe. As for Ortega, he is notoriously private, rarely gives interviews and, unlike fellow billionaires, is known for maintaining a simple lifestyle.

These self-made billionaires, show us the ways that if our desire for success is more than our fear of failure, anything is possible financially in single span of life. What about your financial condition? If it is a struggle, then better for you to take firm actions to improve it because nothing moves in life without action. Now a day unlimited growth is feasible, be it at business or at personal level.

"The real power of money is the power to give it away."
– *N. R. Narayana Murthy*

*****

25. Be Smart with Money! Cash flow is king

There is a huge misconception that most people have about ultra-rich people and money. It's not that these billionaires sit on mountains of money and don't do anything but invent new ways of spending it. Nothing could be further from the truth. Keeping $1 billion (> ₹ 7300 Crore) in cash would cause up to a $135,000 opportunity cost each and every day. It just doesn't make sense. Almost all of the wealth billionaires own is in the companies they own, in the stock of other companies, in real estate, and other assets. Billionaires don't see money as something to spend on themselves. Money is there to invest and create. It is a form of universal energy in a business that allows them to make things happen, to turn their visions into reality.

Learn to Handle Money

Tim Draper learned to invest and understand money as early as age nine.

"My dad got me investing when I was nine years old. I was able to buy one share of a stock with my pocket money. It was Mutual of Omaha.

The stock didn't move much. Then I also put $10 in the bank and watched that, and not much happened to that either. I got 5% a year or something. I think it was 10% a year for a little while. So I thought, "Wow, that's pretty good. It was a dollar, and now it's $1.10."

He got me going early as an investor, and that turned out to have a big impact on me, because when I got started in the venture business, I borrowed money from the SBA, a small business investment company. And when I was trying to borrow the money, I was 26 years old or something, and one of the conditions was you've got to have 10 years of investment experience. I said, "I've been investing since I was 9." The guy goes, "Okay!"

So it helped that I got started early. I think it was great that I had an allowance. Allowance was really important so we understood the value of money. And the job in the garden. I didn't always love working, but I loved getting my penny a minute. I'd always think "a minute went by, I got another penny."

(**Tim Draper** (born 1958) is an American venture capital investor, and founder of Draper Fisher Jurvetson (DFJ), Draper University, Draper Venture Network, Draper Associates, and Draper Goren Holm. His most prominent investments include Baidu, Hotmail, Skype, Tesla, SpaceX, AngelList, SolarCity, Ring, Twitter, DocuSign, Coinbase, Robinhood, Ancestry.com, Twitch, Cruise Automation, and Focus Media.)

Cash Flow is King

Chip Wilson was earning substantial money as an employee starting at 18, but he didn't learn how to handle it properly until he was 20.

"I got a job working on the Alaska oil pipeline, and I was the highest-paid laborer in the world. I was 18 when I went there, maybe even 17, and I made, I think in today's dollars, about $700,000 in about a year and a half. Unbelievable money.

But I worked 18, 19 hours a day, and there was nowhere else to go. I took no time off. I had to leave because I was grinding my teeth. No way to spend the money. But I sent my money back and I bought a house with three suites in it. I lived in one after I came back, and then I rented the other two out, which got me into thinking about cash flow and property.

The big mistake there were I put a down payment on my house, but at that time, interest rates were 19%. So I had all this money in my bank account making me 2% interest, and I'm paying 19% on my mortgage. I didn't understand to shift my money from the bank into my mortgage so I wouldn't have to pay the interest rates. Cash flow is king."

As soon as he solved the problem, the money started to accumulate. This made him wealthy before the age of 25.

(**Chip Wilson** (born 1955) is a Canadian billionaire, businessman, and philanthropist, who has founded several retail apparel companies, most notably yoga-inspired athletic apparel company Lululemon Athletica Inc. Wilson is widely considered to be the creator of the athleisure trend.)

Control Your Spending

Realize that whatever amount you cut your cost, it goes 100% toward your profit, and you would need a multiple of it in revenue in order to earn it otherwise.

Frank Hasenfratz (born 1935) is a Hungarian-born Canadian billionaire businessman, the founder, and owner of the car parts maker Linamar. He started a one-man machine shop in his basement in 1964 and then incorporated it in 1966 under the name Linamar after his two daughters Linda, Nancy, and his wife Margaret.

Frank Hasenfratz is the world champion in cutting costs in the business. After his daughter stepped in as CEO, he focused on his Cost Attack Team (CAT), which he created to do nothing other than finding opportunities to save money within the organization.

You've got to keep in mind, you make let's say 10% profit – if I can save $160,000 here, that took me 1 hour. I've got to make $1.6 million worth of work on the floor to make a $160,000 profit.

Practice cost control and don't spend more than necessary. Frank gets millions in savings for his Linamar company each and every year.

The writer asked Frank to give me an example of a cost-cutting measure.

A silly thing, yesterday. Each machine has a conveyor to take the chips out. We look at the first operation, the conveyor goes, but there's no chips. Very little chips. My assistant Alex said, "Wow, all the conveyors are running, but they're taking small cuts. A conveyor has 5 horsepower. That's roughly 4-kilowatt hour electricity use. A kilowatt-hour is 11 cents, so that's 44 cents, times 24 hours, it's roughly $10 a day. Why not program it? You can program a computer to run the conveyor every 30 minutes for 5 minutes." I said, "You notice anything else? Okay, that's a good one." We have 400 machines there, and $10 a day times 400, you've got $4,000 a day. (Content inspired from 'The Billion Dollar Secret' by Rafael Badziag)

"An investment in knowledge pays the best interest."
- Benjamin Franklin

*****

26. Impact of Association on Financial Life! Observe them carefully...

While associating with people all around us, do we really think that they are impacting several aspects of our life directly or indirectly? This impact is not limited to only personal life but financial life as well. Just have a close look at your associations, is it with positive & successful peoples or with negative & unsuccessful peoples.

Successful people look at other successful people as a means to motivate themselves. They see other successful people as models to learn from. They say to themselves, "If they can do it, I can do it." Modeling is one of the primary ways that people learn.

Why Reinvent the Wheel?

Rich people are grateful that others have succeeded before them so that they now have a blueprint to follow that will make it easier to attain their own success. Why reinvent the wheel? There are proven methods for success that work for virtually everyone who applies them.

Consequently, the fastest and easiest way to create wealth is to learn exactly how rich people, who are masters of money, play the game. The goal is to simply model their inner and outer strategies. It just makes sense: if you take the exact same actions and have the exact same mindset, chances are good you will get the exact same results.

Contrary to the rich, when poor people hear about other people's success, they often judge them, criticize them, mock them, and try to pull them down to their own level of financial life. How many of you know people like this? How many of you know family members like this? The question is, how can you possibly learn from or be inspired by someone you put down?

<u>Dealing with Close Ones</u>

Harv Eker was recently doing a radio interview and a woman called in with an excellent question: "What do I do if I'm positive and want to grow, but my husband is a downer? Do I leave him? Do I try and get him to change? Almost everyone asks the same question: "What if the people I'm closest to aren't into personal growth and even put me down for it?"

Here's the suggested way ahead to these types of questions-

First, don't bother trying to get negative people to change. That's not your job. Your job is to use what you've learned to better yourself and your life. Be the model, be successful, be happy, then maybe...yes maybe—they'll see the light (in you) and want some of it. Again, energy is contagious. Darknesss dissipates in light. People actually have to work hard to stay "dark" when light is all around them. Your job is simply to be the best you can be. If they choose to ask you your secret, tell them.

Second, keep in mind what you want while staying calm, centered, and peaceful. Yes, it's much more difficult to be positive and conscious around people and circumstances that are negative, but that's your test! Just as steel is hardened in the fire, if you can remain true to your values while others around you are full of doubt and even condemnation, you'll grow faster and stronger.

Dealing with Friend or Colleague

If you are going in carpool and now realizing that one of your friends is a negative energy spreader or energy drainer. Now you have a choice! His or her talk might be putting you in an undesirable mindset at the office or at home. You can analyze a similar situation at the lunch table as well.

I have seen, many a time people take flat or house on rent in a society full of negative or unsuccessful people because rent is less there. The advantage of saving the differential amount of rent in a complete year can vanish in minutes in those localities. Your family members, your children can come under the influence of those people & many a time that cost is too high. It is better to have a safe distance from such people, who always have doubt in your growth plan and never feel happy with your progress.

Similarly avoid taking financial or investment advice from people, who are always paying their bills in EMIs & providing you suggestions of loans or debt for any investment. Personally, I had started taking good care of these points for a long time in my life.

Again, energy is contagious: either you affect people or infect people. The same holds true the opposite way around; either people affect or infect you. Let me ask you a question: Would you hug and hold a person you knew had a severe case of measles? Most people would say, "No way, I don't want to catch the measles." Well, I believe negative thinking is like having measles of the mind. Instead of itching, you get bitching; instead of scratching, you get bashing; and also instead of irritation, you get the frustration. Now, do you really want to be close to people like that?

Birds of a Feather Flock Together

You've heard the saying "Birds of a feather flock together." In general, most people earn within 20 percent of the average income of their closest friends? That's why you'd better watch whom you associate with and choose whom you spend your time with carefully.

Rich people don't just join the country club to play golf; they join to connect with other rich and successful people. There's a saying that goes "It's not what you know, it's who you know." If you want to fly with the eagles, don't swim with the ducks! Always try to associate with positive people and disassociate from negative ones. Good things will happen in your life once you become habitual with this logic of association.

Being rich is a right & rich people hang around with winners. Poor people hang around with losers. Why? It's a matter of comfort. Rich people are comfortable with other successful people. They feel fully worthy of being with them. Poor people are uncomfortable with highly successful people. They're either afraid they'll be rejected or feel as if they don't belong. To protect themselves they go into judgment and criticism of rich people's financial life.

Way Ahead

Finally, it's a choice, If you want to improve your financial life, you will have to change your inner blueprint to fully believe you are every bit as good as any rich or ultra-rich out there. Instead of mocking rich people, model them. Instead of shying away from rich people, get to know them. And instead of saying, "Wow, they're so special," say, "If they can do it, I can do it."

Go to the library, a bookstore, or the Internet and read a biography of someone who is or was extremely rich and successful. Henry Ford, Andrew Carnegie, John D. Rockefeller, Mary Kay, Warren Buffett, Jack Welch, Bill Gates, Ratan Tata, Dhirubhai Ambani, Azim Premji are some good examples. Use their story for inspiration, for learning specific success strategies, and most importantly, for copying their mindset to improve your financial life. *(credit to 'Secrets of the Millionaire Mind' by Harv Eker)*

***"You cannot push anyone up a ladder unless he be willing to climb a little himself." –* Andrew Carnegie**

*****

27. How to Reset Self-Limiting Beliefs (About Money)

One of the prominent reasons for our financial success or failure is linked to beliefs, which are stored in our subconscious mind about money. If these beliefs are positive about money, then there is a very high probability to have successful financial life. But if these beliefs are not positive, then most of the time we are in trouble for money. In this case, money is going to be a struggle for us.

Below insightful *EXERCISE* will help you to identify self-limiting beliefs about money & also way ahead to change those beliefs for your financial growth. *(Courtesy 'The Most Powerful Goal Achievement System in the World' by Mike Pettigrew)*

Power of 'Because'

The English language contains a wonderful word that can help you to uncover all sorts of limiting beliefs. That word is "because", and whenever you see the word "because" in a sentence, it is always followed by a reason.

This means you can use the word "because" as a tool to uncover all sorts of reasons – both conscious and subconscious – why you cannot achieve something.

In this exercise, you will be reading a sentence about not being able to succeed financially, and you will be reading that sentence aloud. Then you will write out 10 reasons why you cannot achieve it.

Get the Input from Subconscious Mind

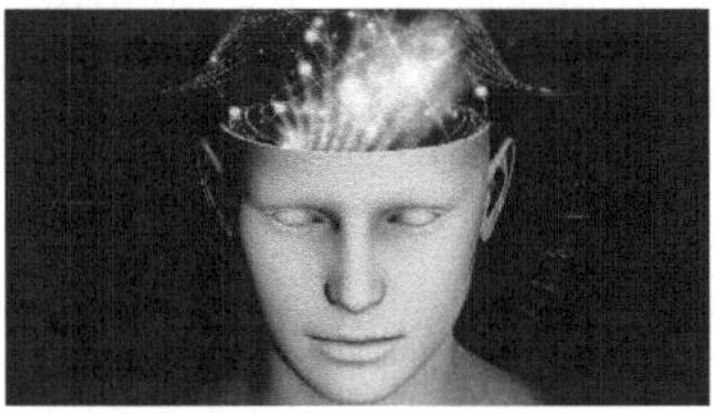

You need to do the first part of this exercise as quickly as you can without really thinking. Don't be logical, just read the sentence aloud, and write down your first reason as quickly as you can. You need to just write down the first thing that comes into your mind, no matter how foolish it may seem. This exercise is not about coming up with logical reasons. Rather, it is an exercise you need to do as quickly as possible, without really thinking, or analyzing, or even judging your reasons. When you do this, some of those reasons will be coming directly from your subconscious mind.

It's your subconscious beliefs and attitudes that we want to reveal in this exercise. If you do the first part of this exercise slowly, then it will not work nearly as well for you.

Exercise Steps

Here are each of the steps in this exercise in more detail, and in this case, we are uncovering limiting beliefs about wealth:

Step 1: Speak the following sentence out loud "I can't become rich because……."

Step 2: Next, as quickly as you can write out a single reason why you can't become rich.

Step 3: Next, speak the same sentence aloud again "I can't become rich because……." and quickly write out another reason why you can't become rich. Repeat this exact same process (of reading the sentence aloud and quickly writing your response) until you have at least 10 reasons.

Step 4: Now look at each of your reasons, and you may be surprised by what they reveal!

If you are currently not rich and you believe it may be difficult to become wealthy, then I'm sure you have written down all sorts of valid reasons why that is so. It's easy to come up with lots of reasons why you can't achieve something, particularly if it's a big, long-term goal.

For example, you might come up with some of the following reasons that could show you the unhealthy attitudes and beliefs you currently hold towards money and wealth.

I can't become rich because:

- Money doesn't grow on trees
- Rich people are greedy
- If I was wealthy, everybody would hate me
- There is only so much to go around
- Money is the root of all evil
- Rich people are smart, and I'm not
- Rich people are arrogant
- It will be too hard to achieve

Please make sure you have at least 10 responses before you complete this first step of the process. If you want to keep going and can come up with more than 10, then it could make this technique even more effective.

Scoring

Next, look at each response that you have written and give yourself a mark from 1 to 10 for each one. If a response has a strong feeling attached to it, then give it a mark between 6 and 10 – the stronger the emotion, the higher your rating. On the other hand, the responses that you don't really believe or that don't have a strong feeling attached to them — mark between 1 and 5.

You are looking for the responses that have the most emotional charge associated with them. The ones that you feel most strongly about, even if you cannot rationally explain why.

So, go through your list of responses and score each one. Those responses that scored between 6 and 10 are most likely the attitudes and beliefs that are currently holding you back the most.

For this example, I have included sample ratings for each response as follows:

I can't become rich because:

- Money doesn't grow on trees SCORE: 1
- Rich people are greedy **SCORE: 7**
- If I was wealthy, everybody would hate me **SCORE: 7**
- There is only so much to go around SCORE: 3
- Money is the root of all evil SCORE: 3
- Rich people are smart, and I'm not **SCORE: 9**
- Rich people are arrogant SCORE: 5
- It will be too hard to achieve **SCORE: 10**

Those highlighted in bold are the scores of four beliefs that could possibly have the greatest emotional charge. Of course, your own scoring may be completely different from the examples.

Create Your List of Opposites

The next step in this technique is to create a new list of responses, but this time you are creating beliefs that are the complete opposite of the previous ones. Also, for this step only select those with the 4 highest scores / the highest emotional charge.

This time, you can take as much time as you like to come up with reasons that counteract those 4 beliefs with the highest emotional charge, as you are no longer trying to draw forth your subconscious beliefs. Rather, you are trying to do the complete opposite - discover logical reasons that will cancel out your limiting subconscious beliefs.

Write out as many opposite reasons as you can for each of these 4 limiting beliefs, and again the more you can come up with the better. The effect that this will have is to loosen the grip these limiting beliefs currently have over you.

Eliminate Those with the Least Emotional Charge

When you have written out these counteracting beliefs for each of your four limiting beliefs with the highest scores, start eliminating those with the least emotional charge.

Remove each one until you have a single powerful empowering belief to counteract each one of your four limiting beliefs.

So, in the previous example, these are the four beliefs with the highest emotional charge. In other words, the limiting beliefs with the most potential negative effects on your life and achievements.

I can't become rich because:

- Rich people are greedy SCORE: 7
- If I was wealthy, everybody would hate me SCORE: 7
- Rich people are smart, and I'm not SCORE: 9
- It will be too hard to achieve SCORE: 10

And here are examples of the best opposite beliefs we have come up with for each of them.

I CAN become rich because:

- Rich people are generous and contribute to society
- When I am wealthy, I will have more time to help others, who will appreciate me
- I can easily learn how other people became rich and copy what they did
- It's easy for me to attract wealth because I choose thoughts of gratitude and abundance

Create Affirmations

The final step in this process is to convert these empowering new beliefs into affirmations that counteract the limiting beliefs that you have uncovered.

Your final list will be very helpful in creating the affirmations that will help you to reprogram your subconscious mind and overcome the limitations that have been holding you back.

These affirmations must be written in the present tense. They also need to be positive, personal, and specific.

Here is one way we can write the empowering beliefs as affirmations:

- I am rich and generous and love contributing to society
- I am wealthy and have lots of time to help others, who appreciate me
- I am learning from rich people and become even richer myself
- I am attracting wealth easily, and I choose thoughts of gratitude and abundance

As these are only examples, you need to do this exercise fully yourself to discover your own self-limiting beliefs about money. You can then create opposite beliefs and convert those beliefs into affirmations that cancel out your limiting beliefs and their effects on your life. <u>Beliefs have the power to control our destiny.</u>

You can do a similar exercise to examine your deep-seated attitudes and beliefs in several other areas to become truly effective and deeply transformational.

"To one who has faith, no explanation is necessary. To one without faith, no explanation is possible."
- *<u>Thomas Aquinas</u>*

*****

28. Money Making Secret (Think & Grow Rich)

The money-making secret with a scientific basis has been described in one of the outstanding books of all time 'Think and Grow Rich' by Napoleon Hill. This book was published in 1937. The principles described in this book are universal and hold true even today.

Andrew Carnegie's Desire

The reason for writing this book is really fascinating and it reveals the secret of making money. This journey of writing this book is very well described by Napoleon Hill himself as below.

"The secret was brought to my attention by Andrew Carnegie (a Scottish-American industrialist and philanthropist) more than a quarter of a century ago. The smart, lovable old Scotsman carelessly tossed it into my mind when I was but a boy. Then he sat back in his chair, with a merry twinkle in his eyes, and watched carefully to see if I had brains enough to understand the full significance of what he had said to me.

When he saw that I had grasped the idea, he asked if I would be willing to spend 20 years or more preparing myself to take it to the world to men and women who, without the secret, might go through life as failures. I said I would, and with Mr. Carnegie's cooperation, I have kept my promise.

Practical Test of Thousands

This book contains the secret, after having been put to a practical test by thousands of people in almost every walk of life. It was Mr. Carnegie's idea that the magic formula which gave him a stunning fortune ought to be placed within reach of everyone who does not have time to investigate how successful people make money. It was his hope that I might test and demonstrate the soundness of the formula through the experience of men and women in every calling. He believed the formula should be taught in all public schools and colleges, and he expressed the opinion that if it were properly taught, it would so revolutionize the entire educational system that the time spent in school could be reduced to less than half.

His experience with Charles M. Schwab and other young associates of Mr. Schwab's type convinced Mr. Carnegie that much of what is taught in schools and colleges is of no value whatsoever in connection with the business of earning a living or accumulating riches. He had arrived at this decision because he had taken into his business one young person after another, many of them with but little schooling, and by coaching them in the use of this formula, developed in them rare leadership. Moreover, his coaching made fortunes for every one of them who followed his instructions.

Even before it had undergone 20 years of practical testing, the secret was passed on to many thousands of men and women who have used it for their personal benefit, as Mr. Carnegie planned that they should. Many have made fortunes with it. Others have used it successfully in creating harmony in their homes.

Secret in Each Chapter

The secret to which I refer is mentioned no fewer than a hundred times throughout this book. It has not been directly named, for it seems to work more successfully when it is merely uncovered and left in sight, where THOSE WHO ARE READY and SEARCHING FOR IT may pick it up. That is why Mr. Carnegie tossed it to me so quietly, without giving me its specific name. If you are READY to put it to use, you will recognize this secret at least once in every chapter. I wish I might feel privileged to tell you how you will know if you are ready, but that would deprive you of much of the benefit you will receive when you make the discovery in your own way.

This secret was used extensively by President Woodrow Wilson during the First World War. It was passed on to every soldier who fought in the war, carefully incorporated or "embedded" in the training he received before going to the front. President Wilson told me it was also a strong factor in raising the funds needed for the war.

A peculiar thing about this secret is that those who once acquire it and use it find themselves literally swept on to success, with what seems to be little effort, and they never again submit to failure! If you doubt this, study the names of those who have used it wherever they have been mentioned, check their records for yourself, and be convinced.

Success Secret to All

The secret serves equally well all who are ready for it. Education has nothing to do with it. Long before I was born, the secret had found its way into the possession of Thomas A. Edison, and he used it so intelligently that he became the world's greatest inventor, although he had but three months of schooling.

The secret was passed on to a business associate of Mr. Edison. He used it so effectively that, although he was then making only $12,000 a year, he accumulated a great fortune and retired from active business while still a young man. It should convince you that riches are not beyond your reach, that you can still be what you wish to be, that money, fame, recognition, and happiness can be had by all who are ready and determined to have these blessings.

Analysis of Well-Known Individuals

While I was performing the more than 20-year task of research which I had undertaken at Mr. Carnegie's request, I analyzed hundreds of well-known individuals, many of whom admitted that they had accumulated their vast fortunes through the aid of the Carnegie secret. Among these individuals were:

HENRY FORD	JOHN D. ROCKEFELLER
WILLIAM WRIGLEY, JR.	THOMAS A. EDISON
JOHN WANAMAKER	FRANK A. VANDERLIP
JAMES J. HILL	F. W. WOOLWORTH
FANNIE HURST	COL. ROBERT A. DOLLAR
GEORGE S. PARKER	EDWARD A FILENE
E. M. STATLER	EDWIN C. BARNES
HENRY L. DOHERTY	ARTHUR BRISBANE

CYRUS H. K. CURTIS	WOODROW WILSON
GEORGE EASTMAN	WILLIAM HOWARD TAFT
THEODORE ROOSEVELT	LUTHER BURBANK
JOHN W. DAVIS	EDWARD W. BOK
MARIE DRESSLER	FRANK A. MUNSEY
ELBERT HUBBARD	KATE SMITH
WILBUR WRIGHT	ELBERT H. GARY
WILLIAM JENNINGS BRYAN	ALEXANDER GRAHAM BELL
DR. DAVID STARR JORDAN	JOHN H. PATTERSON

J. OGDEN ARMOUR	JULIUS ROSENWALD
CHARLES M. SCHWAB	STUART AUSTIN WIER
ERNESTINE SCHUMANN-HEINK	DR. FRANK CRANE
DR. FRANK GUNSAULUS	J.G. CHAPLINE
DANIEL WILLARD	ARTHUR NASH
KING GILLETTE	ELLA WHEELER WILCOX
RALPH A. WEEKS	CLARENCE DARROW

These names represent but a small fraction of the hundreds of well-known Americans whose achievements, financial and otherwise, prove that those who understand and apply the Carnegie secret reach high stations in life. I have never known anyone who was inspired to use the secret who did not achieve noteworthy success in his or her chosen calling. I have never known any person to achieve true professional distinction or to accumulate riches of any consequence, without possession of the secret in one form or another. From these two facts, I draw the conclusion that the secret is more important, as a part of the knowledge essential for self-determination than any which one receives through what is popularly known as "education."

Little Education, But Highly Successful

What is EDUCATION anyway? This will be answered in full detail.

As far as schooling is concerned, many of these individuals had very little. John Wanamaker once told me that what little schooling he had he acquired in very much the same manner as a steam locomotive takes on water, by scooping it up as it runs.

Henry Ford never reached high school, let alone college. I am not attempting to minimize the value of formal education, but I am trying to express my earnest belief that those who master and apply the secret will reach high stations, accumulate riches, and bargain with life on their own terms, even if their schooling has been meager.

Somewhere, as you read, the secret to which I refer will jump from the page and stand boldly before you IF YOU ARE READY FOR IT! When it appears, you will recognize it. Whether you receive the sign in the first or the last chapter, stop for a moment when it presents itself and celebrates—for that occasion will mark the most important turning point of your life.

Only Facts, No Fiction

As you go through this book that it deals with facts and not with fiction, its purpose being to convey a great universal truth through which all who are READY may learn not only WHAT TO DO, BUT ALSO HOW TO DO IT—and receive, as well, THE NEEDED STIMULUS TO MAKE A START.

As a final word of preparation, may I offer one brief suggestion which may provide a clue by which the Carnegie secret may be recognized? It is this: ALL ACHIEVEMENT, ALL EARNED RICHES, HAVE THEIR BEGINNING IN AN IDEA! If you are ready for the secret, you already possess one half of it, therefore, you will readily recognize the other half the moment it reaches your mind."

This is one book, which turned my life in the right direction years back. It's not hard work, but thinking which helps you to improve your financial life. Now at least you are aware of why this book was written. This book is available in many languages, so just grab one and start reading it. From the very beginning, you will find something to implement in your life.

"Whatever the mind of man can conceive and believe, it can achieve." – Napoleon Hill

*****

29. Thinking Leads to Prosperous Life!

We are what we think all the time. It's our thinking, which leads to a different life experience. What is the origin of this thinking? It's mainly our belief system. If we talk about beliefs around money or rich people, positive beliefs lead to a prosperous life and negative beliefs lead to a struggling life.

Fastlane Freedom is working as a belief changer. It's mainly the deep-rooted beliefs in our subconscious mind, which are controlling various aspects of our life. One of the most important aspects is our financial life. Money is like oxygen in today's world. Without money, things get tougher. Money cannot buy happiness, but it can definitely buy the things which make you happy.

It's our beliefs and thinking around these beliefs, which drive our life. If we are having limiting or negative beliefs about money, then our financial life will remain a struggle. This impact is not limited to our own lives, but it also passes to the next generations. There is good news that each one of us can reset self-limiting beliefs about money and change our financial life.

Poor and middle-class people have a negative or limiting thought process about money compare to rich people. This *thinking* comparison has been shared by Steve Siebold in his book titled "How Rich People Think" after more than 20 years of research. This ultimate book helped me a lot to change my own thinking about money and navigating my life in the right direction.

Play It Safe or Take Calculated Risk

Since the masses operate from fear and scarcity-based consciousness, it's logical they would be extremely conservative with money. Their fear is if they lose money they won't be able to make it back. The rich get rich by employing money to attract more without additional effort. They factor in the risks involved in this strategy, knowing that while gains can be sudden and staggering, there will also be losses along the way. Every investor loses money on occasion, but the world-class knows no matter what happens, they will always be able to earn more. The more experienced they become, the smarter they get, and the easier it is to replace money lost in high-risk deals.

So with the downside of taking calculated, educated risks understood and accounted for, they thunder forward like a locomotive searching for financial instruments and lucrative deals that have the power to catapult their net worth and broaden their lifestyle. Security is the watchword of the middle class. Leverage is the watchword of the rich. One group stays awake worrying about losing what they have, while the other can't sleep because they're dreaming of what's possible. The wealthy study their investments like a scientist and are always looking for the gaps missed by the masses that make the difference between a good investment and a bad one. While the middle class is slaving away at jobs and careers every day, dreaming of quitting time and fanaticizing about the weekend, the world-class is employing ideas, people, and money to further expand their financial empire.

Own Money or Other's Money

The majority of the world's population is operating from a consciousness rooted in linear thinking. An example is in their approach to earning money. Linear thinking tells them if they work more hours they'll make more money, and that's true. It's also the most inefficient way to earn more money and another reason most people don't have much.

The rich are masters of non-linear thinking, especially as it relates to money. An example is in how they create an idea they are unable to finance and then proceed to use other people's money to make it happen. The most frequently uttered comment of the middle class in reference to money is "I can't afford it". Rich people know not being solvent enough to personally afford something is not relevant. The real question is, "Is this worth buying, investing in, or pursuing?" If so, the wealthy know money is always available because rich people are always looking for great investments and superior performers to make those investments profitable.

The great ones are aware that it's easier to borrow ten million than ten thousand, a critical non-linear concept to know when raising capital. The middle-class cliché that you have to have money to make money. The truth is you have to have great ideas that solve problems to make money. If you do, you will attract money like a magnet. Money is only an instrument of exchange. Creative ideas are a scarce resource, but most people are so focused on where the money is coming from, that they ignore their ideas, yet the ideas are the only thing that will actually attract the money in the first place! Are you starting to see why a tiny percentage of the population owns the majority of the world's wealth?

Job Security or Outstanding Performance

The average person growing up is bombarded with the same message: *get a good education so you can get a good job*. It is not that there aren't world-class performers who punch a time clock for a paycheck, but for most this is the slowest path to prosperity, promoted as the safest. The truth is, having a job is no safer than owning a business. As counterintuitive as this may seem, people who work for themselves have the power to proactively seek out business and increase revenues at will. If one of their units starts producing revenue, they can simply duplicate this and double the revenue in a short period of time, which is never the case while doing the job.

They can work as many or few hours as they wish and change the direction of the company any time they choose. They are not subject to the whims of management, or the politics of corporate culture. The self-employed are the architects of their own destiny. But while the middle class is attracted to jobs for safety, the world-class knows the only safety any service or product provider has lies in her ability to perform. No matter who signs your paycheck, your financial success will always be based on the level of service you provide and how many people you provide it to. The great ones know there's no such thing as safety in a free market economy. Labor unions, human resource departments, and lawsuits initiated by poor-performing employees are becoming less effective in an increasingly competitive, performance-driven marketplace.

This is where world-class performers seize the opportunity to get rich while the middle class makes a mediocre effort and hides behind the perceived protection of the corporate structure. There are people with jobs who get rich, but the percentage is small. The fastest way to wealth is to work for yourself and determine the size of your own paycheck. The greatest form of security is to have millions in the bank. The rich take advantage of this, while the masses wait on the sidelines, terrified to get in the game for fear they will lose the little money they have. Meanwhile, the world-class is earning more in a year than the average person will make in a lifetime, and the heart of the reason is the unwillingness to let go of a security that does not actually exist.

"No one can become rich without enriching others. Anyone who adds to prosperity must prosper in turn."
- Alexander Orndorff

30. Grow Your Net Worth – Understand the true measure of wealth!

When it comes to money, people in our society typically ask, "How much do you make?" Seldom do you hear the question "What is your net worth?" Recently I tried to ask few people about their net worth. They were not clear on their net worth as the majority of the people only understand the working income.

The true measure of wealth is net worth, not working income. Always has been, always will be. Net worth is the financial value of everything you own. To determine your net worth, add up the value of everything you own, including your cash and investments such as stocks, bonds, real estate, the current value of your business if you own one, the value of your residence if you own it, and then subtract everything you owe. Net worth is the ultimate measure of wealth because, if necessary, what you own can eventually be liquidated into cash.

Component of Net Worth

Rich people understand the huge distinction between working income and net worth. Working income is important, but it is only one of the four factors that determine your net worth. The four net worth factors are:

1. Income
2. Savings
3. Investments

4. Simplification

Rich people understand that building high net worth is an equation that contains all four elements. Because all of these factors are essential, let's examine each one.

Income

Income comes in two forms: working income and passive income. Working income is the money earned from active work. This includes an income from a day-to-day job, or for an entrepreneur, the profits or income taken from a business. Working income requires that you are investing your own time and labor to earn money. Working income is important because, without it, it is almost impossible to address the other three net worth factors.

The more working income you earn, the more you can save and invest. Although working income is critical, again it is only valuable as a part of the entire net worth equation. Unfortunately, poor and many middle-class people focus exclusively on working income, out of the four factors. Consequently, they end up with a low or no net worth.

Passive income is money earned without you actively working. This is another stream of income, which can be used for spending, saving, and investing.

Savings

Savings is also imperative. You can earn wads of money. But if you don't keep any of it, you will never create wealth. Many people have a financial setting in their mind for spending. Whatever money they have, they spend. They choose immediate gratification over long-term balance. Spenders have three mottoes. Their first motto is "It's only money." Therefore, money is something they don't have much of. Their second motto is "What goes around, comes around." At least they hope so because their third motto is "Sorry, I can't right now. I'm broke."

Investments

Once you've begun saving a decent portion of your income, then you can move to the next stage and make your money grow through investing. Generally, the better you are at investing, the faster your money will grow and generate a greater net worth. Rich people take the time and energy to learn about investing and investments. They pride themselves on being excellent investors or at least hiring excellent investors to invest for them. Poor people think investing is only for rich people, so they never learn about it and stay broke.

Simplification

Our fourth net worth factor may well be the "dark horse" of the bunch because few people recognize its importance in creating wealth. This is the factor of "simplification." It goes hand in hand with saving money, whereby you consciously create a lifestyle in which you need less money to live on. By decreasing your cost of living, you increase your savings and the amount of funds available for investing.

To illustrate the power of simplification, here's the story of one of Millionaire Mind participants. When Sue was only twenty-three, she made a wise choice: she purchased a home. She paid just under $300,000 at the time. Seven years later, in a sizzling hot market, Sue sold her home for over $600,000, meaning she profited over $300,000. She considered buying a new home, but after attending the Seminar, she recognized that if she invested her money in a secure second mortgage at 10 percent interest and simplified her lifestyle, she could actually be quite comfortable living on the earnings from her investments and not have to work ever again.

Instead of purchasing a new home, she moved in with her sister. Now, at thirty years of age, Sue is financially free. She won her independence not through earning a ton of money, but by consciously scaling back her personal overhead. Yes, she still works – because she enjoys it – but she doesn't have to. In fact, she only works six months of the year. The rest of the time she spends in Fiji, first because she loves it, and second, she says, her money goes even further there. Because she lives with the locals rather than the tourists, she doesn't spend a lot. It's all because Sue created a simple lifestyle and, consequently, doesn't need the fortune to live on.

Power of Four

Again, building your net worth is a four-part equation. As an analogy, imagine driving a bus with four wheels. What would the ride be like if you were driving on one wheel only? Probably slow, bumpy, full of struggle, sparks, and going in circles. Does that sound familiar? Rich people play the money game on all four wheels. That's why their ride is fast, smooth, direct, and relatively easy.

Poor and most middle-class people play the money game on one wheel only. They believe that the only way to get rich is to earn a lot of money. They believe that only because they've never been there. They don't understand Parkinson's Law, which states, ***"Expenses will always rise in direct proportion to income."***

Here's what's normal in our society. You have a car, you make more money, and you get a better car. You have a house, you make more money, and you get a bigger house. You have clothes, you make more money, and you get nicer clothes. You have holidays, you make more money, and you spend more on holidays. Of course, there are a few exceptions to this rule…very few! In general, as income goes up, expenses almost invariably go up too. That's why income alone will never create wealth.

Track Your Net Worth

Make it a policy to know your net worth to the penny. Here's an exercise that can change your financial life forever.

Take a blank sheet of paper and title it "Net Worth." Then create a simple chart that begins with zero and ends with whatever your net worth objective is. Note your current worth as it is today. Then every ninety days, enter your new net worth. That's it. If you do this, you will find yourself getting richer and richer. Why? Because you will be "tracking" your net worth.

(I am doing this exercise periodically for the last several years. It's helping me to move in the right direction to grow my net worth.)

Remember: what you focus on expands. By tracking your worth, you are focusing on it, and because what you focus on expands, your net worth will expand. Anyway, this law goes for every other part of your life: what you track increases. (Excerpt from book *'Secrets of the Millionaire Mind'* by *Harv Eker*)

"Your mind, more than your actions, determine your net worth."- *Robert Kiyosaki*

*****

31. What Does Money Mean to You? Nurture your relationship with it!

Money has a different meaning to different people. For some, it is a power to choose, for others it is a scare tool. Rich peoples have all positive and broad level meaning with money while middle & poor class people hardly have positive meaning with money. Below keynotes are from the book 'How Rich People Think' by Steve Siebold on the meaning of money.

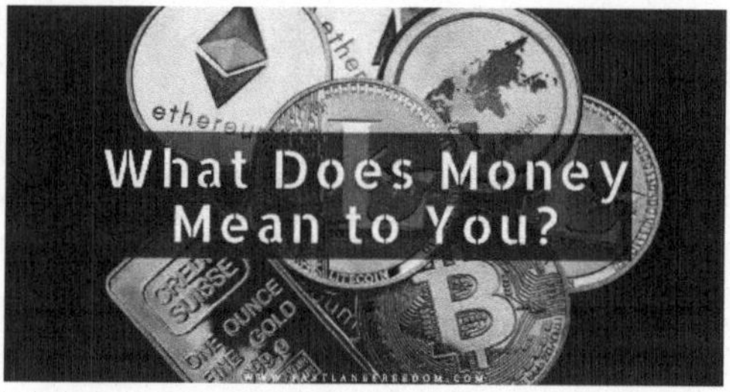

Money, A Critical Component of Life!

The masses take pride in denying the importance of money, and they wear it like a badge of honour. They believe their lack of interest in money tells the world they are above materialism. They deny its importance out of a need to position themselves as morally superior while simultaneously struggling with the fear and terror that comes with being broke. Because they know that their simplicity cannot pay their electricity bill or fees for their children's school. For that, they need only money. It's parallel to a starving man turning away food in an effort to elevate his importance.

Meanwhile, the world-class focus on building net worth, knowing it will offer greater options and opportunities. In a catastrophic health crisis, it may even save their life or the life of someone they love. The great ones are well aware of the critical nature of building wealth, and they are also aware of the limitations of any level of success and financial reward.

The masses are famous for hiding behind the statement "Money won't make you happy," as if this fact somehow forgives them from the responsibility of acquiring it. In 26 years of interviewing the wealthy, Steve Siebold has never had any of them say money is the secret to happiness. Most have said money has little impact on happiness. Money makes you more comfortable, opens doors, and creates opportunities. If the average person directed the amount of mental energy toward earning money as they do worrying about it, they would never have to worry again. The rich are able to re-direct that mental energy toward becoming even richer and sharing their wealth with the less fortunate.

Money, A Friend!

The masses have a broken, adversarial relationship with money. We are taught that money is scarce, hard to earn, and harder to keep. People of influence in childhood instructed them to work hard and hoard as much money as possible. Teachers, coaches, parents, and authority figures, most of whom had little money, conditioned us to see money as a necessary evil.

The world-class has the same childhood experience, but along the way had exposure to a higher thought level that changed the way they think about wealth. They learn that money is not the enemy, but one of their greatest allies and friends. It is a friend that has the power to end sleepless nights of worry, physical pain, and can even save their life. They learn that money is not materialistic; people are materialistic. Money is just a medium of exchange without attachment to anything good or bad.

Nurture Relationship with Money

Blaming money for greed and materialism is like blaming food for making people fat. It's confused thinking. The rich see money as a special friend that can help them in ways no other friend can, and these positive feelings lead them to build a stronger relationship every day. The more money you acquire, the more you understand it, and the more you understand it, the more good you can do with it.

The great ones continue to cultivate and nurture their relationship with money by thinking about how to earn more, invest wiser, and leverage as much as possible. The rich do this so well they often acquire much more money than they'll ever want or need, which is typically when they turn their attention to giving the excess away to charitable organizations. These groups wouldn't survive without the success and generosity of the wealthy who have adopted money as a close friend.

So what is your view? What do you think about money? Is it a critical component in your life or not?

"Money isn't everything... but it ranks right up there with oxygen."- Rita Davenport

*****

32. Habit of Money Management – A process to achieve financial freedom!

Money management! Thomas Stanley, in his best-selling book, *The Millionaire Next Door,* surveyed millionaires and reported on who they are and how they attained their wealth. The results can be summarized in one short sentence: ***"Rich people are good at managing their money."*** Rich people manage their money well. Poor people mismanage their money.

Money Supportive Habits

Wealthy people are not any smarter than poor people; they just have different and more supportive money habits. These habits are primarily based on our past conditioning. So first, if you're not managing your money properly, you were probably programmed not to manage money. Second, there's a better-than-good chance you don't know how to manage your money in a way that's easy and effective. I don't know about you, but where I went to school, nothing related to Money Management was offered. Instead, we learned about several topics, which were not of any use in real life.

It may not be the most glamorous of topics, but it comes down to this: *the single biggest difference between financial success and financial failure is how well you manage your money.* It's simple: *to master money, you must manage money.*

What is First! More Money or Its Management

Poor people either mismanage their money or avoid the subject of money altogether. Many people don't like to manage their money because, first, they say it restricts their freedom, and second, they say they don't have enough money to manage.

As for the first excuse, managing money does not restrict your freedom—on the contrary, it promotes it. Managing your money allows you to eventually create financial freedom so that you never have to work again.

As for those who use the "I don't have enough money to manage" rationale, they're looking through the wrong end of the telescope. Rather than say "when I have plenty of money, I'll begin to manage it," the reality is "when I begin to manage it, I'll have plenty of money."

Saying "I'll start managing my money as soon as I get caught up" is like a heavyweight person saying "I'll start exercising and dieting as soon as I lose twenty pounds." It's putting the cart before the horse, which leads to going nowhere…or even backward! First, you start properly handling the money you have, then you'll have more money to handle.

Story of Triple Scooper

Here is one story, that hits most people right between the eyes. Imagine you're walking along the street with a five-year-old. You come across an ice cream store and go inside. You get the child a single scoop of ice cream on a cone because they don't have any cups. As the two of you walk outside, you notice the cone wobbling in the child's tiny hands and, all of a sudden, plop. The ice cream falls out of the cone onto the pavement.

The child begins to cry. So back you go into the store, and just as you're about to order for the second time, the child notices a colorful sign with a picture of the "triple scooper" cone. The child points to the picture and excitedly screams, "I want that one!"

Now here's the question. Being the kind, loving, and generous person that you are, would you go ahead and get this child the triple scooper? Your initial response might be "sure." However, when considering the question a little more deeply, your final response will be "No." Because why would you want to set the child up to fail? The child couldn't even handle a single scoop, how could the child possibly handle a triple scoop?

The same holds true when it comes to the universe and you. We live in a kind and loving universe, and the rule is "Until you show you can handle what you've got, you won't get any more!"

You must acquire the habits and skills of managing a small amount of money before you can have a large amount. Remember, we are creatures of habit, and therefore the habit of managing your money is more important than the amount.

<u>Way Ahead</u>

To start a money management habit, open a separate bank account designated your Financial Freedom Account

(Investment Account). *Put 10 percent of every penny you receive (after taxes) into this fund.* This money is only to be used for investments and buying or creating passive income streams. The job of this account is to build a golden goose that lays golden eggs called passive income. And when do you get to spend this money? Never! It is never spent—only invested. Eventually, when you retire, you get to spend the income from the fund (the eggs), but never the principal itself. In this way, it always keeps growing and you can never go broke.

Emma's Financial Freedom Story

One of the writer's students, named Emma, recently shared her story. Two years ago Emma was about to claim bankruptcy. She didn't want to; however, she felt she had no other option. She was in debt beyond what she could handle. Then she attended Harv Eker's Seminar and learned about the money management system. Emma said, "This is it. This is how I'm going to get out of this mess!"

Emma, like all the participants, was told to divide her money into several different accounts. "That's just great," she thought to herself. "I don't have any money to divide up!" But since she wanted to try, Emma decided to divide up $1 a month into the accounts. Yes, that's right, only $1 a month.

Based on the allocation system we teach, using that one dollar, she put ten cents into her FFA (Financial Freedom Account). The first thing she thought to herself was "How the heck am I supposed to become financially free on ten cents a month?" So she committed to doubling that dollar every month. The second month she divided up $2, the third month $4, then $8, $16, $32, $64, and so on until the twelfth month was $2,048 that she was dividing up each month.

Then, two years later, she began to collect some amazing fruits from her efforts. She was able to put $10,000 directly into her Investment Account! She had developed the habit of managing her money so well that, when a bonus check of $10,000 came her way, she didn't need the money for anything else!

Emma is now out of debt and on her way to becoming financially free. All because she took action with what she'd learned, even if it was only with $1 a month.

It doesn't matter if you have a fortune right now or virtually nothing. What does matter is that you immediately begin to manage what you've got, and you'll be in shock at how soon you get more. Money miracles will occur once you demonstrate to the universe that you can handle your finances properly. (Excerpt from one of my all-time favorites *'Secrets of the Millionaire Mind'* by *Harv Eker*)

"When money realizes that it is in good hands, it wants to stay and multiply in those hands."- Idowu Koyenikan

*****

33. 55 Interesting Facts About Money - Know the past and present!

Here is the list of interesting facts about money. You might be knowing some of them, but the rest will surprise you!

1. The pound sterling is the world's oldest currency still in use (introduced in the eighth century).
2. The motto on the first US coin was "Mind Your Business" (This wise piece of advice featured on the first one-cent 'Fugio' coin designed by Benjamin Franklin in 1787)
3. The famous "In God We Trust" motto didn't appear on American coins until 1864.
4. Only 8% of the world's currency is in cash (the vast majority of the planet's currency exists in electronic form).
5. The top 1% wealthiest people in the world have 50% of the world's wealth
6. World debt reached a record $281 trillion at end of 2020, more than 355% of global GDP (IIF)
7. No trees are cut down to make our banknotes
8. Star Wars, Pokémon, and Frozen coins are legal tenders on the island of Niue
9. The new English £5 note can play vinyl records
10. A $1 bill lasts just 18 months in circulation
11. In India, the currency has existed in the form of coins since the 6th century BC.

12. Indian Rupee note has Braille signs to help visually impaired people.

13. In India, except for one rupee note and coins, everything else is printed by the RBI.

14. INR at the time of independence was ₹1 = $1

15. The US Bureau of Engraving and Printing uses 9.7 tons of ink a day

16. The average European banknote is home to 26,000 colonies of bacteria (a recent Oxford University study)

17. Queen Elizabeth II features on the most coins and banknotes (featured on the currencies of more than 30 countries)

18. Living people are banned from appearing on US coins or banknotes

19. There is approximately US $37 trillion in circulation: this includes all the physical money and the money deposited in savings and checking accounts.

20. The world's least valuable coin, Uzbekistan's tiyin is worth next to nothing (worth around 2,400 times less than a US one-cent coin)

21. Money is made in factories called mints.

22. Two-thirds of all US$100 bills are held outside the US.

23. There are more than 3.5 million ATMs in the world.

24. The United States officially adopted the dollar as its unit of currency in 1785.

25. The U.S. dollar is the most commonly used currency in the world.

26. The Romans were the first to stamp the image of a living person on a coin.

27. The first paper money was made in China over 1,000 years ago.

28. More Monopoly (game) money is printed each year than actual money.

29. Some countries share a currency (countries in Europe, all use the Euro).

30. In 1920, credit cards were first used in the United States.

31. In The United States, the largest bill ever printed was a $100,000 gold certificate issued in 1934.

32. The International Space Station is the world's most expensive object ever built at US$150 billion.

33. The first Bitcoin transaction was to buy a pizza for 10,000 Bitcoins.

34. Tea bricks were used as money in Siberia until WW2.

35. Over 170 different currencies are used around the world today.

36. One of the most expensive coins in the world is the 1913 Liberty Head nickel (five-cent coin).

37. McDonald's makes about US$75 million per day.

38. Early Romans used salt as a form of money. Even the word "salary" is derived from sal, which means "salt" in Latin.

39. There are three ways by which Governments can get money: 1) print it, 2) borrow it, or 3) collect taxes from their citizens.

40. Abraham Lincoln was the first American pictured on an American coin in 1909.

41. Apple earns US$300,000 per minute.

42. Total U.S. consumer debt is at $14.9 trillion (includes mortgages, auto loans, credit cards, and student loans).

43. The national debt of India amounted to around $2.41 trillion (2020)

44. 37% of all households carry some sort of credit card debt in the United States.

45. 1 in 5 Americans has a zero or negative net worth.

46. Gambling in the U.S. brings in more revenue than theme parks, sporting events, cruise ships, and music combined.

47. The average American pays more than $600,000 in interest over their lifetime.

48. 12% of the money taken home by the average American family is spent on interest.

49. North Korea is the largest counterfeiter.

50. The secret service was originally made to fight counterfeiting in the United States.

51. Before the Federal Reserve in 1913, each bank printed its own money in the United States.

52. A penny costs more to manufacture than it is worth.

53. More than half of lottery tickets sold are bought by 5% of people.

54. Women who wait to marry earn more.

55. If you have $10 in your pocket and you have no debt, you are wealthier than 25% of Americans.

($1 ~ ₹ 74, $1 trillion = $1000 billion, $1 billion = $1000 million)

"Rich people have small TVs and big libraries, and poor people have small libraries and big TVs." - Zig Ziglar

*****

34. Power of Compounding - A Key to Financial Freedom

Power of compounding! It is such a powerful tool that Albert Einstein once called it the most important invention in all of human history. But if it's so awesome, I wondered, why do so few of us take full advantage of it?

Below insightful excerpt on the power of compounding is from one of my favorite books '*MONEY Master the Game: 7 Simple Steps to Financial Freedom*' by Tony Robbins.

#1 Story of Two Brothers

To illustrate the exponential power of compounding, Burton Gordon Malkiel shared the story of *twin brothers William and James,* with investment strategies that couldn't have been more different. Malkiel (born August 28, 1932) is an American economist and writer most noted for his classic finance book *A Random Walk Down Wall Street.*

The story supposes that William and James have just turned 65—the traditional retirement age. William got a jump-start on his brother, opening a retirement account at the age of 20 and investing $4,000 annually for the next 20 years. At 40, he stopped funding the account but left the money to grow in a tax-free environment at the rate of 10% each year.

James didn't start saving for retirement until the ripe old age of 40, just as his brother William stopped making his own contributions. Like his brother, James invested $4,000 annually, also with a 10% return, tax-free, but he kept at it until he was 65—25 years in all.

In sum, William, the early starter, invested a total of $80,000 ($4,000 per year × 20 years at 10%), while James, the late bloomer, invested $100,000 ($4,000 per year × 25 years at 10%).

Difference…It's 600% More!

So which brother had more money in his account at the age of retirement?

Tony knew where Malkiel was going with this, but he told the story with such joy and passion that it's like he was sharing it for the very first time. The answer, of course, was the brother who'd started sooner and invested the least money. How much more did he have in his account? **Get this: 600% more!**

In Malkiel's example, it was **William, the brother who'd gotten the early start and stopped saving before his brother had even begun, who ended up with almost $2.5 million. And it was James, who'd saved all the way until the age of 65, who had less than $400,000. That's a gap of over $2 million!** All because William was able to tap into the awesome power of compounding for an additional 20 years, giving him an insurmountable edge—and saddling him with the family dinner checks for the rest of his life.

#2 Story of Benjamin Franklin's $1,000

Not convinced that compound interest, over time, is the only sure way to grow your seed of money into the bumper crop of financial security you'll need to meet your future needs?

Malkiel shared another favorite story to bring home his point—and this one's from our history books. When Benjamin Franklin died in 1790, he left about $1,000 each to the cities of Boston and Philadelphia. His gift came with some strings attached: specifically, the money was to be invested and could not be touched for 100 years. At that point, each city could withdraw up to $500,000 for designated public works projects. Any remaining money in the account could not be touched for another 100 years. Finally, 200 years after Franklin's death, **a period of time that had seen stocks grow at an average compounded rate of 8%,** each city would receive the balance—**which in 1990 amounted to approximately $6.5 million.** *(Image Credit Wikipedia)*

Imagine that $1,000 grows to $6.5 million, with no money added over all those years. How did it grow? Through the power of compounding! Yes, 200 years is a long, long time—but a **3,000% rate of return** can be worth the wait.

Malkiel's examples show us what we already know in our hearts to be true: that for most of us, our earned income will never bridge the gap between where we are and where we really want to be. Because earned income can never compare to the power of compounding!

#3 Story of an Ordinary Employee

Theodore Johnson, whose first job was with the newly formed United Parcel Service in 1924, worked hard and moved his way up in the company. **He never made more than $14,000 a year, but here's the magic formula: he set aside 20% of every paycheck he received and every Christmas bonus, and put it into company stock.** He had a number in his head, a percentage of income he believed he needed to save for his family—just as you will by the end of this chapter—and he committed to it. Through stock splits and good old-fashioned patience, **Theodore Johnson eventually saw the value of his UPS stock soar to over $70 million by the time he was 90 years old.**

#4 Story of a Sixth-Grade Educated Women

Have you heard the story of Oseola McCarty from Hattiesburg, Mississippi—a hardworking woman with just a sixth-grade education who toiled for 75 years washing and ironing clothes? She lived simply and was always careful to set aside a portion of her earnings. "I put it in savings," she explained of her investment philosophy. "I never would take any of it out. And I just put it in. It just accumulated." *(Image Credit Wikipedia)*

Oh, boy, did this woman's money accumulate. **At 87 years old, McCarty made national news when she donated $150,000 to the University of Southern Mississippi to start a scholarship fund.** She became The University of Southern Mississippi's (USM) most famous benefactor. She worked hard and knew enough to see that her money worked hard, too.

"I want to help somebody's child go to college," she said—and she was able to do just that, on the back of her good diligence. There was even a little leftover for a small luxury item: she bought an air conditioner for her house.

<u>Just Do This!</u>

I was not aware of this compounding power, at least 8-9 years back. But at the same time, I continued doing investments. Today I could realize the power of compounding.

I was sharing the above concept with one of my colleagues, who is doing regular investment. I also explained to him the power of compounding with mathematical formulas. He was fascinated by seeing this as there was a tremendous difference in net amount by changing the investment amounts and rate of return. Within three days, he had double his yearly investment amount. I liked it!

Remember, when your money starts earning money for you, you are heading towards financial freedom.

"Money makes money. And the money that money makes, makes money."- Benjamin Franklin

*****

35. Overcome the Fear of Failure & Build a World Class Life!

What differentiates the middle-class from world-class, when we talk about money? It's their thinking. Instead of creating means to earn more money, they are dependent on others. They have sleepless nights to worry about money to pay the next installment or bill. With a fear of failure in mind, it is almost impossible to think big and fulfill your wish. In such situations our subconscious mind work against our plans. And this fear-based thinking keeps away middle class from money or wealth.

They hesitate to take any risk, if they take, they fail because they still have fear of failure in mind. Fear is one of the most powerful emotions and you might be knowing that our subconscious mind works based on emotions and feelings. So instead of helping us to make our plan successful, it works against our plans.

Below excerpt from 'How Rich People Think' will help you to understand the thinking of rich and middle-class people. You can change your mindset accordingly. This book was written after more than 20 years of research by Steve Siebold.

Waiting for Ship or Building Your own!

The average person subconsciously believes he's going to be discovered, saved, or made rich by an outside force in the future. It's like the fat person slowly killing herself through obesity, who patiently waits for the next pill or tonic to make her thin and healthy. They are convinced their hero on the white horse is right around the corner ready to save them from themselves.

The world-class knows no one is coming to their rescue, and if their life is going to be uncommon in any way, it will be through their own efforts. The foundational principle they live by is self-reliance and personal responsibility. They're not counting on the government to bail them out or their family to take care of them in their old age. Champions don't wait for things to happen, they make things happen. The more physical, mental, emotional, and spiritual effort they invest in, the more help they receive from others who have traveled the same path. Self-made man/woman is only self-made in the sense that they proactively began chasing their dream with no expectation of assistance.

Living Beyond or Below Your Means!

The average person spends more than they make because they make so little. How can a family survive on the average income and still save money? Instead of getting creative, most people try to do more with less and suffer sleepless nights worrying about the future. The middle class is the wealthiest sub-group of the working poor, and most of them live beyond their means because they earn so little. These people aren't stupid; on the contrary, some are smarter and better educated than members of the world-class. The difference lies in their focus. The middle class focuses on everything but getting wealthy because they have so many limiting beliefs about money and what being wealthy means, it's the last thing they want to think about. Then they listen to so-called financial gurus who criticize them for overspending on silly things.

The rich live below their means, not because they're so savvy, but because they make so much money they can afford to live like royalty. It's easy to live below your means when you earn more in a day than most people earn in a year. Not to mention that the rich earn money primarily through leverage, and not hard labor. It's hard labor that creates the physical and psychological stress that kills so many poverty, working, and middle-class workers. Here's how to live below your means and tap into the secret wealthy people have used for centuries: ***get so rich you can afford to***.

Money as Stress or Peace of Mind!

The average person would rather think about anything but money with the negative feelings they associate with it. They see money as a never-ending necessary evil that must be endured as part of life. The world-class sees money as the great liberator, and with enough of it, they are able to purchase financial peace of mind. The great ones know money can't solve every problem or eliminate every worry, but it does have the power to reduce stress in tough times while providing opportunities in good times. The rich believe if you can write a check for a problem and make it go away, you don't have a problem. Money makes most problems disappear. The masses have been worrying about money since the beginning of time, and they always will. Not because they're not capable of acquiring wealth, but because they're operating in a fear-based consciousness that keeps them broke.

The lack mentality of the masses attracts them to focus their thoughts on how many ways they can stretch a dollar.

Meanwhile, the rich are focused on how they can earn more, invest more effectively, and leverage their money. Notice how few discounts are offered at high-end retailers and upscale establishments. It's not that the rich don't like getting good deals and discounts, but they are generally more interested in making quantum leaps in their net worth than they are in pinching pennies. The secret the rich know that the masses don't is that being rich is more about consciousness than currency. Most people never break out of middle-class mediocrity because of their level of thinking. Getting rich begins by thinking rich. It's about what's happening inside your mind, but the masses are so fearful and skeptical they fail to grasp this simple truth.

Think Small or Think Big!

The masses are at a level of consciousness that dictates they pay attention to every detail and petty problem. They are more interested in gossip, drama, and other people's problems than they are in their own success. This level of thought consumes massive amounts of mental energy, and by the end of the day, they have little left for creative thought and problem-solving.

The world-class purposely ignores the small thinking, ego-based personality problems that plague the middle class. They know they only have so many units of mental energy available each day, and they choose to focus all of them on thinking big. They are happy to exchange the small life of survival for the big life of abundance. The great ones are operating at a level of consciousness where fear doesn't exist. It's a level of thought that allows them to focus on their ultimate vision. At this level of thought, anything seems possible. Every dream that seems crazy to the masses looks surprisingly doable. The world-class know the key to success in anything is reaching a higher level of awareness.

In other words, the masses don't earn $50,000 a year because they want to; they earn $50,000 a year because they're not aware of how to earn $500,000. Professional athletes are better than amateurs because they're operating at a higher level of awareness in their sport. It's all about raising your level of conscious awareness. And it begins by releasing any fear-based thoughts that enter your mind and clear of the small-minded, petty thinking of the masses.

"He that waits upon fortune, is never sure for dinner."
- Benjamin Franklin

*****

36. Subconscious Mind and Wealth - Understand This Strong Connection!

When you are not well-off, then it's very difficult to convince subconscious mind that you will always have plenty of wealth. On one side you are struggling to make ends meet and on another side, you are wishing for more than the required wealth. You want your subconscious power to develop on your wish. Before that wish passed to the subconscious mind, your own consciousness creates obstacles by showing you the current reality.

There are men and women around you, who work a few hours a week and making fabulous sums of money. Do not believe the story that the only way you can become wealthy is by hard labor. It is not so; the effortless way of life is the best. Do the thing you love to do and do it for the joy and thrill of it.

Wealth is simply a subconscious conviction on the part of the individual. You will not become a millionaire by saying, "I am a millionaire, I am a millionaire." You will grow into a wealth consciousness by implementing ideas of wealth and abundance.

(Excerpt is from one of my all-time favorite "The Power of Your Subconscious Mind" by Joseph Murphy, which was first published in 1963.)

Invisible Means Of Support

The trouble with most people is that they have no invisible means of support. They seem helpless when business falls away, the stock market drops, or they lost their investments. The reason for such insecurity is that they do not know how to tap the subconscious mind. They are unaware of the inexhaustible storehouse within.

A man with a poverty-type mind finds himself in poverty-stricken conditions. Another man with a mind filled with ideas of wealth is surrounded by everything he needs. It was never intended that man should lead a life of pennilessness. You can have wealth, everything you need, and plenty to spare. Your words have the power to cleanse your mind of wrong ideas and to inculcate the right ideas in their place.

Method to Build A Wealth Consciousness

This is what you should do: Repeat for about five minutes to yourself three or four times a day, *"Wealth – Success."* These words have tremendous power. They represent the inner power of the subconscious mind. You are not saying, "I am wealthy," you are dwelling on real powers within you. There is no conflict in the mind when you say, "Wealth." Furthermore, the feeling of wealth will well up within you as you dwell on the idea of wealth.

The feeling of wealth produces wealth; keep this in mind at all times. Your subconscious mind is like a bank, a sort of universal financial institution. It magnifies whatever you deposit or impress upon it whether it is the idea of wealth or of poverty. Choose wealth.

"Use the power of your conscious and subconscious mind to create a vibrational match for the abundance you desire and deserve." – Jack Canfield

Why Affirmations For Wealth Fail

Joseph Murphy shared the experience of his talk to many people during the past thirty-five years whose usual complaint is, "I have said for weeks and months, 'I am wealthy, I am prosperous,' and nothing has happened." He discovered that when they said, "I am wealthy, I am prosperous," they felt that they were lying to themselves.

One man told him, "I have affirmed that I am prosperous until I am tired. Things are now worse. I knew when I made the statement that it was obviously not true." His statements were rejected by the conscious mind, and the very opposite of what he superficially affirmed and claimed was made manifest.

Your affirmation succeeds best when it is specific and when it does not produce a mental conflict or argument; hence the statements made by this man-made matter worse because they suggested his lack. Your subconscious accepts what you really feel to be true, not just idle words or statements. The dominant idea or belief is always accepted by the subconscious mind.

Avoid Mental Conflicts

The following is the ideal way to overcome this conflict for those who have this difficulty. Make this practical statement frequently, particularly prior to sleep: *"By day and by night I am being prospered in all of my interests."* This affirmation will not create any argument because it does not contradict your subconscious mind's impression of financial lack.

The above suggestion was taken up by one businessman whose sales and finances were very low and who was greatly worried. He sits down in his office, becomes quiet, and repeats this statement over and over again: "My sales are improving every day." This statement engaged the cooperation of the conscious and subconscious mind; results followed.

How to Make It Happen

You might be saying, "Oh, I did that and nothing happened." You did not get results because you indulged in fear thoughts perhaps ten minutes later and neutralized the good you had affirmed. When you place a seed in the ground, you do not dig it up. You let it take root and grow. Suppose, for example, you are going to say, "I shall not be able to make that payment." Before you get further than, "I shall..." stop the sentence and dwell on a constructive statement, such as, *"By day and by night I am prospered in all my ways."*

Your subconscious mind is never short of ideas. There is within it an infinite number of ideas ready to flow into your conscious mind. These ideas will appear as cash in your wallet in countless ways. This process will continue to go on in your mind regardless of whether the stock market goes up or down, or whether the value of the rupee goes up or down. Your wealth is never truly dependent on bonds, stocks or money in the bank; these are really only symbols necessary and useful, of course, but only symbols.

The point to emphasize is that if you convince your subconscious mind that wealth is yours and that it is always circulating in your life, you will always and inevitably have it, regardless of the form it takes.

Control Envious Emotion

'Envy' is one emotion that keeps many people away from wealth. For example, if you see your neighbor or friend depositing large sums of money in the bank and you have only a small amount to deposit, does it make you envious? The way to overcome this emotion is to say to yourself, *"Isn't it wonderful! I rejoice in that man's prosperity. I wish for him greater and greater wealth."*

Entertaining envious thoughts is devastating because it places you in a very negative position; therefore, wealth flows from you instead of to you. If you are ever annoyed or irritated by the prosperity or great wealth of another, repeat immediately that you truly wish for him or her greater wealth in every possible way. This will neutralize the negative thoughts in your mind.

Way Ahead (A Lullaby)

As you go to sleep at night, practice the following technique. Repeat the word, "Wealth," quietly, easily, and feelingly. Do this over and over again, just like a lullaby. Lull yourself to sleep with the one word, "Wealth." You should be amazed at the result. Wealth should flow to you in avalanches of abundance. Your subconscious mind will dwell on "Wealth" and suggest you some actions. Just go ahead and take those actions. Sometimes it's not your first action, which will give you results but series of such actions sure!

*****

37. Is Your Money Working Hard for You?

Who is working hard in your life? Is it you or your money? If it's money, then enjoy your life. If it's you, then transform your hard-earned money to work for you.

No question, working hard is important, but working hard alone will never make you rich. Look around the real world. There are millions—no, make that billions—of people who slave away, working hard all day and even all night long. Are they all rich? No! Are a lot of them rich? No! Most of them are broke or close to it. On the other hand, whom do you see lounging around the country clubs of the world? Who spends their afternoons playing golf, tennis, or sailing? Who spends their days shopping and their weeks vacationing? They are Rich people! So let's get this straight: the idea that you have to work hard to get rich is bogus!

"Your economic security does not lie in your job; it lies in your own power to produce—to think, to learn, to create, to adapt. That's true financial independence. It's not having wealth; it's having the power to produce wealth."
- Stephen Covey

There is one quote, which goes like "a dollar's work for a dollar's pay." But it forgot to tell us what to do with that "dollar's pay." Knowing what to do with that dollar is where you move from hard work to smart work. Rich people can spend their days playing and relaxing because they work smart. They use leverage tools extensively. They employ other people to work for them and their money to work for them.

<u>Work Energy to Money Energy</u>

You have to work hard for your money. For rich people, however, this is a temporary situation. For poor people, it's permanent. Rich people understand that "you" have to work hard until your "money" works hard enough to take your place. They understand that the more your money works, the less you will have to work.

Consider money as a form of energy. Most people put work energy in and get money energy out. People who achieve financial freedom have learned how to substitute their work energy with other forms of energy. These forms include other people's work, business systems at work, or investment capital at work.

Each one of us has a goal to become "financially free" as quickly as possible. Definition of financial freedom is simple: it is the ability to live the lifestyle you desire without having to work or rely on anyone else for money. You become financially free when your passive income exceeds your expenses.

Harv Eker has identified two primary sources of passive income. The first is "money working for you." This includes investment earnings from financial instruments such as stocks, bonds, money markets, mutual funds, as well as owning mortgages or other assets that appreciate in value and can be liquidated for cash.

The second major source of passive income is "business working for you." This is a business where you do not need to be personally involved for that business to operate and yield an income. Examples include rental real estate; royalties from books, music, or software; licensing your ideas; becoming a franchisor; owning storage units; owning vending or other types of coin-operated machines; and network marketing, to name just a few. It also includes setting up any business under the sun that is systematized to work without you.

Why is Creating Passive Income Difficult?

Without passive income, you can never be free. But, and it's a big but, did you know that most people have a tough time creating passive income? There are three reasons. First, conditioning. Most of us were actually programmed not to earn passive income. When you were somewhere between thirteen and sixteen years old and you needed money, what did your parents tell you? Did they say, "Well, go out there and earn some passive income?" Doubtful! Most of us heard, "Go to work," "Go get a job," or something to that effect. We were taught to "work" for money, making passive income abnormal for most of us.

Second, most of us were never taught how to earn passive income. In my school, Passive Income was another subject that was never offered. Since we didn't learn about creating passive income structures in school, we learned it elsewhere, right? Doubtful. The end result is that most of us don't know much about it, and therefore don't do much about it.

Finally, since we were never exposed to or taught about passive income and investing, we have never given it much attention. We have largely based our career and business choices on generating working income. If you understood from an early age that a primary financial goal was to create passive income, wouldn't you reconsider some of those career choices?

Unfortunately, almost everyone has a money blueprint that is set for earning working income and against earning passive income.

Long-Term & Short-Term Thinking

Rich people focus & think long-term. They balance their spending on enjoyment today with investing for freedom tomorrow. Poor people focus & think short-term. They run their lives on immediate gratification. Poor people use the excuse "How can I think about tomorrow when I can barely survive today?" The problem is that, eventually, tomorrow will become today; if you haven't taken care of today's problem, you'll be saying the same thing again tomorrow too.

To increase your wealth, you either have to earn more or live on less. Nobody is putting a gun to your head telling you the house you have to live in, the kind of car you have to drive, the clothes you have to wear, or the food you have to eat. You have the power to make choices. It's a matter of priorities. Poor people choose now, rich people choose balance.

Again, the idea is to have your money work as hard for you as you do for it, and that means you have to save and invest rather than make it your mission in life to spend it all. It's almost funny: rich people have a lot of money and spend a little, while poor people have a little money and spend a lot. Rich people buy assets, things that will likely go up in value. Poor people buy expenses, things that will definitely go down in value. Rich people collect land. Poor people collect bills.

Create Freedom Fighters

I have shared my own experience of real estate investment with many people. Just "buy real estate, especially land." It's best if you can purchase property that can produce positive cash flow, but as far as I'm concerned, any real estate is better than no real estate. Sure, real estate has its ups and downs, but in the end, be it five, ten, twenty, or thirty years from now, you can bet it will be worth a heck of a lot more than it is today, and it could be all you need to get rich. As the saying goes, ***"Don't wait to buy real estate, buy real estate and wait."***

While poor people see a dollar/rupee as a dollar/rupee to trade for something they want right now, rich people see every dollar/rupee as a "seed" that can be planted to earn a hundred more dollars/rupees, which can then be replanted to earn a thousand more dollars/rupees. Think about it. Every dollar/rupee you spend today may actually cost you a hundred dollars/rupees tomorrow. Consider each of your dollars/rupees to be investment "soldiers," and their mission is "freedom.".

(Excerpt is inspired from book "Secrets of the Millionaire Mind" by Harv Eker.)

38. Change Limiting Beliefs About Money (from Scarcity to Abundance)

There is a vast difference between the beliefs of the masses and the world-class about money. If we are optimistic, then we never find any pessimistic person around us, but if we are pessimistic, then we never find any optimistic person around us. How amazing is it? You may see the universe supporting or conspiring against you to achieve your financial goals.

Different Level of Consciousness in World

The masses see life through fear and scarcity. This group believes the world is a tough place, and some people will always try all the means to cheat them. If you're not careful, people will take what you have. Such thoughts continuously run in the mind of these people. As fear is one of the most strong emotions and it blurs the hope of financial abundance. People with fear-based thinking see the world as a non-supporting place and easily turn themselves as pessimistic. If at all they get support from other people, they think that there must be some hidden advantage to the person who is helping them.

The world-class see the universe in their support to achieve the goals. Once they were also having pessimistic thought process like the masses, but slowly they change the track & choose to become optimistic. With a positive and growth mindset, they get the support of the universe. They became aware of the benefits of controlling their thoughts. The rich choose to see the world as it is, but at the same time *as it can be.* They see the positive side of people and also visualize a child inside the adult. They see the untapped potential of everyone they interact with. And they see all of this because they made an optimistic choice. The rich have a commonly held belief that the universe, God, or a higher power is right there with them, actively at work guiding them along the path of their ultimate vision of abundance to support millions of people.

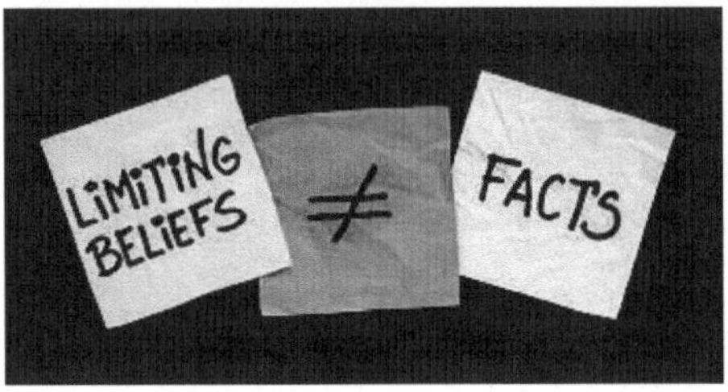

They swiftly move toward their goals and dreams believing they are being guided at every turn. While many fear-based thinkers believe people are out to get them, but the world-class believe the world is in their corner cheering them on and helping them along the way. In the same world & same reality; there is a different level of consciousness.

Non-linear Thinking Leads to Great Fortune

The average person thinks of money in a linear term. To earn more money they need to work for more hours. As there are only 24 hours in a day, so their earning cap is fixed. Insite of having several real-life examples of people who have generated a fortune from zero in single life, they ignore it. They think of it as a case of plain luck. They do not want to understand the mechanism behind it.

They've been trained to believe by others in the middle-class consciousness that the longer you work the more money you will make. The linear line of thought is the only condition the masses understand. If a corporate employee wants to make more money, his or her first thought is to get an MBA. In the linear term, more education equals more money. More hard work means more money, in reality, this is the most inefficient method of making money.

 # Fact of the day: In the world, more than 70% of ***billionaires*** *are self-made. #*

The rich know big money originates in a non-linear way. Even without knowing the above fact, just look around in your society or city, you will find such self-made rich people. It requires letting go of everything you think you know about earning money and making space for a higher level of thought. The rich are masters at taking a single idea and leveraging it so many ways that it's difficult to identify its point of origin.

The masses think about how much they can get paid for doing something, which may not be necessarily of their interest. But the rich people figure out what they love to do and then find out how to make money doing it. The goal of money is the same, but the road they travel is just opposite to achieve it. One is the linear path and the other is non-linear. One is all about money and the other is filled with enthusiasm, joy, and passion. Who would you bet on to earn more? For the masses, linear thinking is unrelated to making money. For world-class, non-linear thinking is the epicenter of every great fortune.

Power of Beliefs

The masses have a deep-rooted belief that wealth, prosperity, and great success are only for few people who have extreme talent, specialized knowledge, or luck. The middle class struggles because they expect it. When they achieve uncommon success or get what they want unexpectedly, they're convinced it's a trick and their good fortune won't last. And it happens in reality. They could not able to reset their financial thermostat & soon reach their original financial position. For example, if one person is managing 500K annually and suddenly he gets 5000K by some means. Within few months or a few years, he will lose his extra 4500K and come to the original level of 500K. Years of middle-class programming have created this losing cycle that usually follows them to the end.

The world-class has the polar opposite belief that success, fulfillment, and happiness are the natural order of existence. This single belief drives the great ones to behave in ways that virtually guarantee their success. While the masses are playing video games, watching television, and surfing the internet, champions are setting goals and designing strategies to make them a reality. It's never like the masses are not having the desire to succeed, but their belief system holds them back from making it big.

After all, why should I stretch myself dreaming of being rich when I don't believe it's possible for me? While the rich appear more ambitious, it's actually their belief that drives them to succeed, and the more they succeed, the stronger their belief grows. They are on an upward spiral of success, while the masses are on a downward spiral of mediocrity. (Blog is inspired by one of my favorite books "How Rich People Think" by Steve Siebold.)

"Don't limit yourself. Many people limit themselves to what they think they can do. You can go as far as your mind lets you. What you believe, remember, you can achieve." —Mary Kay Ash

*****

39. The Best Cashflow Quadrant Reviewed - Analyse Your Quadrant!

The Cashflow Quadrant represents the different methods to generate income or money. Your income stream or income level is not necessarily linked to your level of education. There is no doubt that higher education can give you an early advantage but it's not responsible for your final destination in terms of finance.

Many successful people have left school without receiving a college degree—people such as Thomas Edison, founder of General Electric; Henry Ford, founder of Ford Motor Co.; Bill Gates, founder of Microsoft; Ted Turner, founder of CNN; Michael Dell, founder of Dell Computers; Steve Jobs, founder of Apple Computer; and Ralph Lauren, founder of Polo. A college education is important for traditional professions, but not for how these people found great wealth. They developed their own successful businesses.

<u>What Is the Cashflow Quadrant</u>

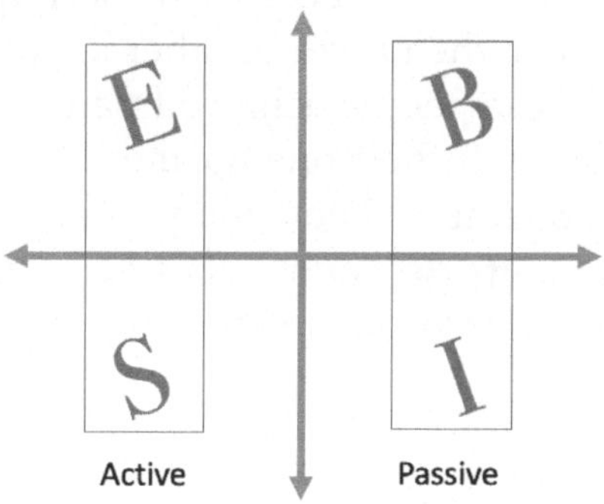

E (Employee): You exchange your time and effort for an income. If you don't work, you will not get income.

S (Self-employed or Small Business): You work for yourself, but can you take a 6-week holiday and your business keeps on working without you?

B (Big Business): These group people have peoples working hard for them to generate them an income

I (Investor): They are the people that have money working hard for them. Play golf and enjoy a good life.

E & S cashflow quadrants are mainly active sources of income. Without your own involvement, you cannot generate money. But the majority of the people belong to these two quadrants. These people take a minimum or no risk and security is their prime focus. It's mainly job or regular paycheck security, which holds them back. They know if they are jobless for a few months, life will be too hard as they will not be able to pay various EMIs, children's fees, etc. They are surrounded by so many securities, that most of them cannot even think beyond their routine job. This is the main reason that these groups remain in these quadrants for life long and even pass an almost similar legacy to their next generation.

The other two cashflow quadrants i.e. B & I are mainly passive sources of income. People in these quadrants enjoy freedom by leverage the power of other people and money to work for them. These people achieve financial freedom in the fastest way possible. If their one business is established, they hop for another business. They enjoy leisure time and make their best investments decisions. These quadrant people also pass an almost similar legacy to their next generation.

"I would rather earn 1% off a 100 people's efforts than 100% of my own efforts."- John D. Rockefeller

Which Quadrant is Your Source of Income?

The cashflow quadrant represents the different methods to generate income or money. For example, an employee earns money by holding a job and working for a person or a company. Self-employed people earn money working for themselves. A business owner owns a business that generates money, and investors earn money from their various investments—in other words, money generating more money.

People have income sources from one quadrant or multiple quadrants at a time. For *employees* at an early stage for their career, it starts with E, and then progressively there are E & I quadrants. For *Self-employed* people at the early stage, it's S, and then progressively there area S & I quadrants and possibly can I as well. And for *Big business* group people it's mainly B & I. And for the Investor group, it's mainly I & B.

Each quadrant of income generation requires different frames of mind, different technical skills, and different educational paths. While money is all the same, the way it's earned can be vastly different. If you begin to look at the four different labels for each quadrant, you might want to ask yourself, "Which quadrant do I generate the majority of my income from?"

One Can Earn Income in All Four Quadrants

Most of us have the potential to generate income from all four quadrants. Which quadrant you or I choose to earn our primary income from is not so much dependent upon what we learned in school. It's more about who we are at the core—our beliefs, values, strengths, weaknesses, and interests.

Regardless of what type of work we perform, we can still work in all four quadrants. Like for an engineer following can be the cases-

Quadrants	As an Engineer
E	Join the staff of any private or government organization.
S	Open a consulting firm in his or her specialized field or start making products in a workshop with very limited manpower.
B	Start a business, employing several people. Establishing it and then leveraging it.
I	Become an investor in someone else's business or in vehicles like the stock market, bond market, and real estate.

The important words are "generate income from." It's not so much what we do, but more how we generate income.

Different Methods of Income Generation

More than anything, it's the internal differences of our core beliefs, values, strengths, weaknesses, and interests that affect which quadrant we decide to generate our income from. Some people love being employees, while others hate it. Some people love owning companies but don't want to run them. Others love owning companies and also love running them. Some people love investing, while others can't get past the risk of losing money. Most of us are a little of each of these characters. Being successful in the four quadrants often means redirecting some internal core values and resetting limiting beliefs.

It is important to note that you can be rich or poor in all four quadrants. There are people who earn millions and people who go bankrupt in each of the quadrants. Being in one quadrant or another does not necessarily guarantee financial success.

Decide Your Own Quadrant

By knowing the different features of each quadrant, you'll have a better idea as to which quadrant, or quadrants, might be best for you. It's is not where you have started from, the important is where you are destined to.

If you want to achieve financial freedom, then it's always advisable to join the group of quadrant B & I people.

As stated earlier, there is no guarantee for financial security in any of the quadrants, then why should not we try for the right side of the quadrants instead of the left side of the quadrants. For most people working on the left side of the quadrant, there are few legal tax breaks available. But by working to generate income on the right side of the quadrants, one can acquire money faster and keep that money working for oneself longer without losing large chunks of it in the form of taxes. (Excerpt From 'Rich Dad's CASHFLOW Quadrant' by Robert T. Kiyosaki)

*****

40. The Relationship Between Time and Money -It's Not Strictly Linear!

Time and Money! We all know that time is inherently limited. But if we are having a similar thought process for money, then we are living in a false world.

'Money is limited in the world', this is the prime base for traditional retirement and personal finance advice. The vast majority of personal finance advice out there is focused on cutting back and spending less. It doesn't acknowledge the simple truth that money is limited only if you don't try to make more of it.

Money is inherently infinite. It's a human invention, and as long as people are helping the economy grow by working, spending, and investing, governments can print more money to keep up. There is and always has been a massive gap between those who have a lot of money and those who don't. But in theory, there is enough money in the world for everyone to have all the money they need.

The problem is, many people don't take advantage of available opportunities. They accept whatever money they are given—generally whatever their companies are willing to pay—without considering other ways to make more money. They say they want to make more money but spend all their free time binging on smart TV with many subscriptions, gaming, surfing, etc.

When we believe that money is scarce, we end up sacrificing a great deal of time in order to make and save it. And unlike money, *time is inherently limited.* If we believe money is scarce, we will spend precious time trying to save it when we actually don't have to. We'll spend hours clipping coupons or hunting for a deal online just to save a few bucks off our bill.

The same goes for earning money: every minute we spend trying to make money is a minute we can't use to do something else—it's gone forever.

"A man who dares to waste one hour of time has not discovered the value of life." - Charles Darwin

Available time with us

Most people work between 70,000 and 80,000 hours over the course of their careers. Even these stark numbers don't tell the whole story. Standard working hours of countries worldwide are around 40 to 44 hours per week. If we add in time for commuting, that's about 50 hours. There are 168 hours in a week, so after you subtracting 50 hrs and also about 56 hours for sleeping, you left with 62 hours.

That sounds like a lot—more than double what you spend working in a week—but consider that not all hours are equally valuable. Studies have shown that we are most alert and energetic early in the day, but that's the time we're usually working. By the time we get off the clock, we're usually so tired or run down from working all day and commuting that we don't want to do anything except sit on the couch. This is why the average watch time of TV is around 2.8 hrs per day across the world & lead by America as 4.5 hrs per day.

We have weekends, but how often do we spend those running around trying to catch up on all the shopping and chores we didn't get to during the week? The point is, we are trading the best hours of our week and our life for money. Many a time it happens even when people do not love their work. There is a huge difference between working at a job you hate, being stuck at a desk or on the clock for forty or more hours a week, and doing work you love and are passionate about, on your own time, and having the freedom to do something else if you want to.

Power of compounding

It's *your TIME,* so take control of it. If you take advantage of opportunities to make the most of your money, you can save a lot more money and correspondingly even more time. Every penny invested today is worth hours, if not days, of your freedom in the future. The more you save today, the more time you buy in the future.

The earlier you start and the more you save, the sooner you will reach financial independence. This strategy will rapidly decrease the number of years and the amount of money you need to reach financial independence. Remember: The key to fast-tracking financial freedom is to make and invest as much money as early and frequently as you can. Actually, it happens with the power of compounding interest.

Albert Einstein once described compound interest as the "eighth wonder of the world," saying, *"he who understands it, earns it; he who doesn't, pays for it."* Compound interest is when the interest one earns on a principal balance is reinvested and generates additional interest. Click here to learn more about the power of compounding with real-life examples.

Infinite Possibilities

Fortunately, the relationship between money and time is not strictly linear. If you want to make more money, you don't necessarily need to sacrifice more time to do so. You don't have to be limited by your own hours or even the hours in the day. You don't have to look far to find examples of people who can work half as many hours to earn twice as much money as someone else, and it's not always because they are smarter or more experienced, or work in a more lucrative field. Even you can find people who make money by trading very little, if any, of their own time because they've invested a lot of time up-front in building consistent long-term income streams.

People who invest their money in the stock market, real estate, etc. get leisure time in life as their money is working hard to earn money 24×7. This is known as a passive source of income because they don't have to actively do anything to earn it, and it is the ultimate money-making strategy. What's better than being able to make money doing literally nothing? Even the best part is they get relatively more time to evaluate their investment plans to get the best returns.

Once you reach the point where you no longer have to trade your time for money, you can choose to spend that time however you please. When you have enough (or even just close to enough!), you can quit the higher-paying job you hate to take a lower-paying one that is meaningful to you. You can explore, grow, give back, follow your passions, and find new passions. You can travel the world, pick up a new hobby, learn a new skill, volunteer—the possibilities are infinite. *(Excerpt is from 'Financial Freedom' by Grant Sabatier)*

*****

41. Reasons Why Continuous Learning Makes You Rich

Can continuous learning makes you rich? Basically, there are three most dangerous words in the English language. Those words are "I know that." So how do you know if you know something? Simple. If you live it, you know it. Otherwise, you heard about it, you read about it, or you talk about it, but you don't know it. Put bluntly, if you're not really rich and really happy, there's a good chance you still have some things to learn about money, success, and life.

If things are not moving the way they should, then it's time to introspect. You might be thinking that you know it all, but the reality might be different. When "know it all" is not working then it's time to implement "learn it all." Things will start changing from that moment onwards.

<u>If You Think Education is Expensive, Try Ignorance</u>

There's a saying that author and speaker Jim Rohn uses: "If you keep doing what you've always done, you'll keep getting what you've always got." You already know "your" way, what you need is to know some new ways i.e. new thinking, new actions, and therefore new results. That's why it's very important you continue to learn and grow.

There is nothing in this world as static. Everything alive is constantly changing. Take any plant. If a plant isn't growing, it is dying. It's the same with people as well as all other living organisms: if you are not growing, you are dying. Similarly, if you're not continuously learning, then you will be left behind.

Poor people claim they can't afford to get educated due to a lack of time or money. On the other hand, rich people relate to Benjamin Franklin's quote: "If you think education is expensive, try ignorance." You might have heard this before, "knowledge is power," and power is the ability to act.

To improve your financial life, you need to learn the skills and strategies to accelerate your income, to manage money, and to invest it effectively. The definition of insanity is doing the same thing over and over and expecting different results. Look, if what you've been doing were working, you'd already be rich and happy. Anything else your mind raises up as a response is nothing more than an excuse or justification.

Every Master was Once a Disaster

Success is a learnable skill. You can learn to succeed at anything. If you want to be a great golfer, you can learn how to do it. If you want to be a great piano player, you can learn how to do it. If you want to be truly happy, you can learn how to do it. If you want to be rich, you can learn how to do it. It doesn't matter where you are right now. It doesn't matter where you are starting from. What matters is that you are willing to learn.

An Olympic skier shared his story in Harv's session. He told everyone the story of how when he was a kid, he was the worst skier of all his buddies. How they sometimes wouldn't call him to go skiing with them because he was so slow. To fit in, he went to the mountain early each weekend and took lessons. Pretty soon he not only kept up with his buddies, but he also surpassed them. He then got involved in the racing club and learned from a top-ranked coach. His exact words were "I might be a master skier now, but I definitely started out as a disaster. You can learn to succeed at anything. I learned how to succeed at skiing, and my next goal is to learn how to succeed with money!"

Nobody is Born Genius

No one comes out of the womb a financial genius. Every rich person learned how to succeed at the money game, and so can you. Remember, your motto is, if they can do it, I can do it!

Becoming rich isn't as much about getting rich financially as about whom you have to become, in character and mind, to get rich. The fastest way to get rich and stay rich is to work on developing you! The idea is to grow yourself into a "successful" person. Remember, your outer world is merely a reflection of your inner world. You are the root; your results are the fruits.

If you grow yourself to become a successful person, in the strength of character and mind, you will naturally be successful in anything and everything you do. You will gain the power of absolute choice. You will gain the inner power and ability to choose any job, business, or investment arena and know you'll be a success. When you are a level 5 person, you get level 5 results. But if you can grow into a level 10 person, you will get level 10 results.

If you don't do the inner work on yourself, and somehow you make a lot of money, it would most likely be a stroke of luck and there's a good chance you'd lose it. But if you become a successful "person" inside and out, you'll not only make it, you'll keep it, grow it, and most importantly, you'll be truly happy.

BE-DO-HAVE or HAVE-DO-BE

Rich people understand the order to success is BE, DO, HAVE. Rich people understand, "If I become a successful person, I will be able to do what I need to do to have what I want, including a lot of money."

Poor and middle-class people believe the order to success is HAVE, DO, BE. Poor and most middle-class people believe "If I have a lot of money, then I could do what I want and I'd be a success."

Here's something else only rich people know: the goal of creating wealth is not primarily to have a lot of money, the goal of creating wealth is to help you grow yourself into the best person you can possibly be. In fact, that is the goal of all goals, to grow yourself as a person. World-renowned singer and actress Madonna was asked why she kept changing her persona, her music, and her style every year. She responded that music was her way to express her "self" and that reinventing herself each year forces her to grow into the kind of person she wants to be. In short, success is not a "what," it's a "who." The good news is that "who" you are is totally trainable and learnable.

Be the Experts in Your Field

Another key difference between rich people and poor and middle-class people is that rich people are experts in their fields. Middle-class people are mediocre in their field, and poor people are poor in their field. How good are you at what you do? How good are you at your job? How good are you at your business? Look at your paycheck. That will tell you everything. It's simple: to get paid the best, you must be the best.

We recognize this principle in the professional sports world every day. Generally, the best players in every sport earn the most. They also make the most money on endorsements. This same principle also holds true in both the business and financial worlds. Whether you choose to be a business owner, a professional, whether you're in commissioned sales or a salaried job, whether you're an investor in real estate, stocks, or anything else, all things being equal: the better you are at it, the more you'll earn. This is just another reason why being a continuous learner and enhancing your skill in whatever arena you are in is very important.

On the topic of learning, it's worth noting that rich people not only continue to learn, but they also make sure they learn from those who have already been where they themselves want to go. Rich people take advice from people who are richer than they are. Poor people take advice from their friends, who are just as broke as they are.

Just as there are successful paths to climbing Mount Everest, there are proven routes and strategies for creating high income, fast financial freedom, and wealth. You have to be willing to learn them and use them.

(The excerpt is from "Secrets of the Millionaire Mind" by Harv Eker.

*****

42. How to Increase Your Ability to Earn More Income?

There is one simple question for you about your income. Can you earn twice as much money as you do now in the same amount of time? Can you earn three times as much money? Ten times? Is it possible that you could earn 1,000 times the amount of money you do now in the same amount of time? Absolutely!—if you find a way to be worth 1,000 times more to your company or your fellow man.

Below insightful excerpt is from one of my favorite books 'Awaken the Giant Within' by Anthony Robbins.

Become More Valuable

The key to wealth is to be more valuable. If you have more skills, more ability, more intelligence, specialized knowledge, a capacity to do things few others can do, or if you just think creatively and contribute on a massive scale, you can earn more than you ever thought possible. The single most important and potent way to expand your income is to devise a way to consistently add real value to people's lives, and you will prosper. For example, why is a doctor paid more than a doorman? The answer is simple: the doctor adds more value. He has worked harder and developed himself so that he is worth more in terms of his capacity to add measurable value to people's lives. Anyone can open a door. A doctor opens the doors of life.

Why are successful entrepreneurs so well rewarded financially in our culture? It's because they add more value than virtually anyone around them.

> ***"All wealth comes from adding value, from producing more, better, cheaper, faster, and easier than someone else."***
> ***- Brian Tracy***

Add Values

There are two primary benefits that entrepreneurs create. First, they obviously add value to their customers by increasing the quality of their lives through the use of their products. This, by the way, is critical for any company to prosper. So often, companies forget that their real purpose for being is not just to make a profit. While a profit is an absolute must for a company to survive and flourish—like eating or sleeping, a necessity—it's not the real purpose.

The true purpose of any corporation is to create products and services that increase the quality of life for all the customers they serve. If this is achieved on a consistent basis, then profit is absolutely assured. However, a company can profit in the short term and not be here in the long term if it doesn't continually add value to people's lives. This holds true for corporations as much as individuals.

The second thing that entrepreneurs do is that, in creating their products or services, they create jobs. Because of these jobs, the employees' children can go on to higher education and become doctors, lawyers, teachers, social workers, and add more value to society as a whole—not to mention the fact that these families spend the money that they earn with other vendors. The chain of value is never-ending. When Ross Perot was asked for the secret of his wealth, he said, "What I can do for this country is create jobs. I'm pretty good at that, and Lord knows we need them." The more value you contribute, the more you will earn if you put yourself in the position to do so.

The lesson is simple. You don't have to be an entrepreneur to add more value.

Expand Your Knowledge

But what you must do every day is to continually expand your knowledge, your skill, and your ability to give more. This is why self-education is so critical.

If you want to earn more money where you are today, one of the simplest ways to do so is to ask yourself, "How can I be worth more to this company? How can I help it to achieve more in less time? How could I add a tremendous amount of value to it? Are there some ways that I could help cut costs and increase quality? What new system could I develop? What new technology could I use that would allow the company to produce its products and services more effectively?" If we can help people to do more with less, then we truly are empowering others, and we will be empowered economically as well, as long as we put ourselves in a position to do so.

In sessions, participants brainstorm ways they can add more value and therefore increase their income. The key question to ask yourself is: How could I help touch more lives? How could I do it at a deeper level? How could I give a better quality of product or service? Inevitably, some people will say, "There's no way that I could add more value; I'm already working sixteen hours a day as it is!" Remember, there is no suggestion to work harder or even work smarter. The point is, what new resources could you employ that could add more value to other people?

#1 Real Example

A massage therapist who was one of the most successful in his field, and he wanted to know how he could increase his earnings when he was booked solid. He couldn't see one more person a day, and he was already charging the highest rates in his field. As he began to brainstorm new ideas, focusing on how he could take the resources he had to help his patients and others, he began to realize that if he could team up with someone who owned a physical therapy unit, and refer his patients who needed help, he could receive a referral fee.

His income is now almost double, working the same number of hours a day. All he did was find a way to add more value to both his doctors and his clients. Since he knew the doctors well, and they understood his form of therapy, there was a greater consistency of care between them, and he benefited financially in the process.

#2 Real Example

In another area, one of the top radio salespersons is a woman whose primary marketing strategy is not merely to sell radio time, but to constantly look for opportunities to help local companies prosper. For example, the minute she hears that a new shopping center is going to be built, she contacts potential vendors for the shopping center and lets them know about the opportunity, allowing them to get a jump on the market. She then contacts the developer and introduces herself as a radio station representative who works with people in their industry all the time. Would the developer like to see a list of the top vendors in their fields?

Out of this strategy, several things result. She's adding value beyond the radio time people would purchase to promote their companies. She's found a way to give them much more than anyone else around, so they usually buy a significant portion, if not all, of their radio time from her. This motivates them to reciprocate value for value. This does not require a great deal of her time, but it makes her more valuable to her customers than any other radio salesperson in the region, and her income reflects it.

#3 Real Example

Even if you work in a large corporation, you can add more value. There was a woman working as a claims processor for a hospital. She saw how slowly things were going and, knowing that claims processing was the economic lifeline of the hospital, she discovered that she could be much more efficient and potentially process four to five times as many claims as she had previously. She asked her supervisors if she could do the work of five people, would they increase her salary by 50 percent? They said that if she proved she could consistently produce results over a period of time, they would do so. Since then, not only has she increased job efficiency and her income, she has a newfound sense of pride.

The key to increasing your income with your company is remembering that you can't just increase the quality of what you're doing by 50 percent and expect a 50 percent increase in income. A company must profit. The question to ask yourself is, "How can I increase the value of what I do by ten to fifteen times?" If you do this, in most cases you'll have no trouble increasing your income.

*****

43. What Do You Think : More Money More Stress or Less Stress!

More money more stress or it's not like that! What is your thinking? The average person believes high income equals high stress. Successful, high-energy, goal-driven people are often seen as fast-moving and hard-driving, which makes them appear as though they are living a stressful existence. College students are often advised to focus their studies on a field that will allow them to earn a respectable salary while still being able to enjoy their life, implying that making big money will make them miserable. This is one typical piece of advice that each and every middle-class kid receives from parents, teachers.

The world-class believes the more money you make the less stress you will have, because 'not all' but most problems can be solved by writing a check. Most stress created in business and in relationships is caused by a lack of money, so the more financial resources you have the less stress you will experience. The rich often make the point that if you want to eliminate stress and spend more time with your family the most expeditious path is to get rich enough to quit your job.

Many corporate employees earning six-figure salaries and a bevy of bonuses are actually part of the working class poor because they spend more than they make all the while worrying about not having sufficient time with their family. These otherwise intelligent people rarely realize that with a few adjustments in their belief system and behavior they could earn more money in a week than they currently earn in a year. The belief that blocks them is they think the only way to earn more money is through more hours, harder work, or promotion. They believe money is made in a linear fashion which limits what they can earn.

The people that embrace non-linear approaches to building wealth have the world at their fingertips. They are in control of how much they earn and how much stress they expose themselves to. The secret to ascending to this level is realizing that it will take a different set of beliefs and philosophies to make it happen.

"Money is only used for two things. One, to make you comfortable, and the more comfortable you are the more creative you will become. And the other purpose is it enables you to extend the service you provide far beyond your own presence." - Bob Proctor

More Money More Problem or Less Problem!

After more money more stress, let's take another myth. Among the masses is the idea that millionaires are workaholics overloaded with so many problems they don't have time to enjoy life. This is another excuse the masses use to justify being broke. It's as if they're looking for a reason to avoid success by making it seem unattractive. While it's true many millionaires appear to be workaholics, for most, it's because they love what they do and don't consider it work. There's a fine line between work and play for the self-made rich, and they often struggle to make the distinction. These people enjoy solving problems because they're in love with their occupation and fascinated with its dynamics.

When you're a millionaire and tired of solving problems, you pay someone else to solve them for you. The masses don't have that option, so in reality, the average person is faced with the prospect of having to solve more problems in a day than many world-class performers do. The ability to pay other people to solve problems frees them up to focus on more important and profitable areas of their business. Money gives the rich control over every aspect of their business, and many areas of their lives. The more money they have, the fewer problems they have to personally address.

While the masses are staying up at night because they're overloaded with so many problems, the millionaires are fast asleep knowing everything will be taken care of. The curious paradox is the sleep-deprived middle-class performer is worrying about all these problems, and barely making enough money to survive, while the millionaire isn't worried at all and makes a fortune. This has been happening for several centuries, and the middle class continues to deny the significance of being rich.

The Rich Obsessed with Money or Success!

The average person believes obsession is a bad word. The truth is wealthy people have a healthy obsession with getting what they want, which includes money. Materialism is only part of their motivation, the strongest for most is the freedom to do what they want, when they want. The world-class sees business and life as a game, and it's a game they love to win. This is the reason millionaires still go to work every day chasing their next success. Money to these people is no more than a gauge that tells them when they have achieved their latest target. Most of the money the rich earn will be passed down to heirs or charity.

It's difficult to be obsessed with money you're never going to spend. It's more about success and accomplishment. And it's not that there's anything wrong with being obsessed with wealth, it just isn't the primary motivator for most millionaires after they reach a certain net worth. This number is different for everyone, but the phenomenon is the same. Winners love to win, and the elation they experience after victory never gets old.

The masses don't understand this because they've never had enough money to make it a secondary priority in their lives. It's hard to see life as a game when you can't pay your phone bill. The rich are masters at getting what they want, and their number one objective is building a substantial net worth so they can shift their focus to higher-level pursuits, such as personal fulfillment, time freedom, and philanthropy. This enables them to live a lifestyle most people only dream about and experience a level of personal satisfaction most can't even imagine.

(Excerpt from 'How Rich People Think' by Steve Siebold, who had done research of more than 20 years on rich people and middle-class people thinking.)

"The biggest risk is not taking any risk. In a world that is changing really quickly, the only strategy that is guaranteed to fail is not taking risks."- Mark Zuckerberg

*****

44. The Best Habits of Wealth - Followed by Self-Made Billionaires!

In the long term, your habits determine your future. You first need the foundation of the following habits of wealth if you want to be really successful in business. (Excerpt is from 'The Billion Dollar Secret: 20 Principles of Billionaire Wealth and Success' by Rafael Badziag.)

Habit 1: Get Up Early

Getting up early is the number one common habit of the most successful entrepreneurs. Why is getting up early so important? There are several advantages. Early hours, when the world awakes to life, have something of primal energy around them. You may have felt this energy at the sunrise. You have time for yourself, time to think in silence, and time to work undisturbed. This, coupled with your fresh mind and body, makes you extremely productive during these hours. And you get this great feeling of doing something, of progressing when others are still asleep. It can even propel you through the rest of the day, giving you an additional energy boost.

But keep in mind: It's not the short sleep that makes you successful in business. It's getting up early. Some billionaires sleep for three hours only, some need as much as eight hours, but all of them get up early. Those that need to sleep longer just go to bed earlier.

Habit 2: Keep Healthy

Whether in business or in life in general, health is extremely important. Without health, life is a misery and no amount of success will make it better for you. There is no point in doing business if you aren't healthy. Jack Cowin *(a Canadian-Australian businessman and entrepreneur with long-term involvement in franchised fast-food chains in Australia and Canada)* once gave a speech with the title "If I knew then what I know now" with 13 different points. *"The first one is, if you lose your health, nothing else matters. Your health is the most important. I don't care how wealthy or how important you are or how much power you've got; if you lose your health, nothing else counts. So you've got to look after your health. Include techniques such as meditation or physical training into your life to maintain your mental and physical health."*

Habit 3: Read

Books are the treasure of the world's knowledge. When Rafael asked Cho Tak Wong *(a Chinese entrepreneur, the chairman of Fuyao Group, one of the largest glass manufacturers in the world)* about one message he would like to give to the world audience, his answer was: *"I'd ask the young people to read books, read a lot of those about how to do things right, how to be a good person."*

Keep in mind, Cho Tak Wong was expelled from elementary school and was illiterate at the age of 14. He never graduated from any school and learned to read and write all by himself. He is a self-taught person who gained all his knowledge from the books he read and the experiences he made. This was what allowed him to become the World Entrepreneur of the Year 2009, the best entrepreneur in the world, so to say. Reading is, together with exercise, the activity that billionaires spend time on regularly. They usually read in the morning before they go to the office. Some read also before they go to sleep.

Habit 4: Routines and Rituals

Billionaires take time during the day to spend it alone to think. Some do it by meditating; some do it during other activities like sports.

Routines and rituals are sets of habits that, when employed consistently, will in the long term inevitably produce profound results. Ritualized habits are easier to keep and thus more sustainable. The long-term application brings about a compound effect. Unfortunately, bad rituals like a cigarette break also will produce profound results but on the negative side. That's why it's essential to set up and follow routines and rituals that support your objectives.

"Starting the Business Day"

Routine Billionaires have their usual way to start their day in the office. It's a routine that they follow automatically the minute they enter their office. What you do first depends very much on the type of business you are involved in and of course the scale of your business. Frank Stronach *(an Austrian and Canadian businessman and politician)* explains it using manufacturing as an example:

When you are small, you go to the factory. When you are larger, you start with your secretary: "What's new? Anything urgent?" Then you might meet an executive committee or whatever. So it depends on what stage. I went through all these stages.

Chip Wilson *(a Canadian billionaire, businessman, and philanthropist)* approaches every day in a systematic way. Asked what is the first thing he does in the office, he says:

I sit down and I think about what my number one priority of the day is. What is my goal to get done for that day? And I look at my calendar and go, "Okay, is my calendar right?" Actually, do that the night before, so I rearrange things. Then I go, "Has anything changed between last night and this morning, and what do I need to do?" I need to actually insert it into my calendar to give me time to do it.

Habit 5: Discipline

All the billionaires interviewed by Rafael are self-made billionaires and the most disciplined people. They put a high standard on themselves and on the people around them. In sports, you can achieve results only if you are disciplined to train consistently. Similarly in business, you can achieve results only if you are disciplined to apply yourself consistently to what needs to be done. You have to show up day in, day out for decades to make it happen. But billionaires are by no means superhumans or perfect working automatons. They also sometimes feel lazy just like you and me. The only difference is: they are aware of this fact and they don't let themselves slack. They take up the struggle to overcome their weaknesses.

This is what Michał Sołowow confessed to Rafael: *I wake up every morning and do things I don't like. I force myself to do them every day. Because I am not hardworking, I force myself to do hard work. I am not systematic, so I have to force myself to become systematic.*

"The chains of habit are too light to be felt until they are too heavy to be broken." —Warren Buffett

*****

45. How To Be Ready with High Income Skill

Table of Contents

In recent times you might have noticed that traditional jobs are disappearing faster and faster? There are plenty of low income skill jobs vs high income skill jobs in the market. Have you seen the news about technology and robots replacing more and more workers? Did you know that fewer and fewer workers can secure full-time jobs? The old ways of working are disappearing.

In the past, you could graduate from college, land a secure job, work with the same company at the same job for forty years, and then retire from there only. That's no longer the case, and you might already know that. Maybe there's no way you'll be staying at one company for forty years, or perhaps you've had to switch careers multiple times already, or maybe you know someone laid off recently and had to face the unforgiving job market.

Skill Economy

The old "job economy" is steadily disappearing, and a new economy is emerging; it's called the Skill Economy.

Fewer full-time jobs are available in the job market.

The available full-time positions are way too expensive for companies to keep.

Let's talk about the first one: there are fewer full-time jobs available than in the past. Have you seen the kiosks that are replacing cashiers at McDonald's? Most of the time you get recorded answers with lot of options when you called into a call center? Haven't you heard the stories about companies going through "corporate downsizing"- basically where they fire many people?

The world is changing. Regular full-time jobs are becoming less and less available. Companies are only keeping high-level executives and high-touch members as full-time staff—everything else can be automated, outsourced, or contracted. Not only that, but the full-time jobs that do remain are becoming too expensive for companies to keep. At each and every step of the corporate ladder, people can be replaced. It can be their call or company call.

Now, if you were running a company, would you pay 20-30 percent more for an employee who does the same amount of work as another employee? Think about it in terms of your life. If you were buying a car, and two dealers offered you the same car—same brand, same model, same condition—and one dealer quotes you $20,000 while the other quotes you $26,000, which would you choose? Of course, you'd go with the $20,000 car, the less expensive option. This is the same decision many companies are now making.

With full-time jobs disappearing, contract work and freelance work are emerging, fueling the Skill Economy. People are being paid more and more based on their skills, not their credentials, experience, or job position. However, not all skills are created equal—some reward you better than others.

Low and High Income Skills

You're probably familiar with the concept of "supply and demand"—when there is high demand and low supply for something, it is more valuable; when there is low demand and high supply for something, it is less valuable.

It works the same way with skills. The principle of supply and demand divides skills into two categories: Low Income Skills and High Income Skills. Low Income Skills are high in supply and low in demand—that is why they will give you low pay. They are a commodity, and there are many more people out there who have these skills than there is a demand for them.

As an example, imagine a person working as a cashier. The wage of this person will be less but he or she had to work long tough hours. His or her income (paychecks) didn't reflect their efforts. Why was that? It's because working as a cashier is a Low Income Skill. No matter how good or fast they are in their work but they could always be replaced by anyone on the street.

In contrast to Low Income Skills, High Income Skills are low in supply and high in demand—that's why they will give you higher pay. If you have a High Income Skill, people will fight to hire you, because you can deliver high value. Plus, if you have a High Income Skill, the work you get will offer you much more compensation, flexibility, and happiness. In addition, you'll get the ability to control your finances, the time you work, and the location of your work. These are all crucial factors in deciding your happiness at work.

High Income Skills are low in supply and high in demand; this means low-level skills like grocery shopping, mopping floors, and driving are NOT High-Income Skills. That's why people who work as delivery boys on food-based apps or working as a driver of rental taxi apps won't likely make a very high income per month. There is nothing wrong with being in that profession. It's great for many people. It gives them flexibility and to earn outside of regular work hours. However, these people likely won't make a high income because they are replaceable. If one driver or delivery boy isn't available, there were dozens waiting around the corner.

Avoid This Mistake While Developing High Income Skill

A few years ago, Charlie Rose interviewed Will Smith and asked about his secret to success. Here's what he replied:

"You don't set out to build a wall. You don't say, 'I'm going to build the biggest, baddest, greatest wall that's ever been built.' You don't start there. You say, 'I'm going to lay this brick as perfectly as a brick can be laid.'"

Will Smith perfectly described how to stack your High-Income Skills: succeed with one High-Income Skill first, then move on to the next. This way, you'll build a High-Income Skill stack. Most people develop High-Income Skills in the wrong direction. They will try one skill for a while, and then jump to the next, and then jump to the next before even developing slight competency with their current skill. Instead of building a wall like Will Smith described, they are making a brick pile.

You may go through times that are tough when developing your High-Income Skill. Maybe you'll reach a plateau, or perhaps you'll struggle with finding people who will pay for your skill. The mistake people make too often is abandoning the High-Income Skill they have been working on when results don't come quickly. Dan Lok's advice for people who want to change course: be patient. Wait until you can earn $10,000 a month with your first High Income Skill before moving to the next. (Article is inspired from "Unlock It: The Master Key to Wealth, Success, and Significance" by Dan Lok)

*****

46. Level of Your Thinking Defines the Level of Your Wealth!

The level of your thinking is directly proportional to the level of your wealth. If you got out of bed in the morning and went to work because you wanted to, you are in control of money. If you got out of bed in the morning because you had to, money is in control of you.

Across the world, 99% of the population is being controlled by money. The effect is a lack of money. The cause is thinking. Albert Einstein once said, "a problem cannot be solved at the level of consciousness in which it occurs." Knowing this, champions raise their level of consciousness by studying how the world class creates wealth.

Role of Formal Education

The middle class believes formal education is the answer to acquiring wealth, yet very few academics are wealthy. They seek advanced degrees and certifications and are confounded when these things don't bring them riches. While the great ones are strong advocates of higher education, they don't believe it has much to do with acquiring money.

The middle class trades time for money. The world class trades ideas that solve problems for money. Money flows like water from ideas. The middle class often scorns the world class out of frustration over a lack of money. Ideas and it's execution, this is such a simple concept that the majority misses it.

The poverty class talks about the past; the middle class talks about other people, and the world class talks about ideas. Professional performers know money doesn't care which direction it flows. They know the world will bend over backward to make them rich if it will help them solve their problems.

What About a Million-Dollar Opportunity!

About 150 years ago, Karl Marx was sure the working class, as a whole, would rise up and overcome oppression if they had a chance. What Marx didn't figure into the equation was the poverty-driven thought process of the people. Give people operating at middle-class consciousness a million-dollar opportunity, and they will find a way to make it back to the middle class. It is where their limited self-image tells them they belong. The difference has nothing to do with reality. It's all perception in the mind of the performer.

If you want to become wealthier, begin by raising your self-image by upgrading the self-talk you use regarding money and finances. If all you do is chase more money, you are simply attacking the effect. The cause is how you think, and if you improve the cause, the effect will take care of itself.

You might have heard or read news related to popular TV show winners. They become winners with a hefty amount of money but within five years of time, the majority of them come to their original level. It became almost impossible for them to expand their thinking in line with their winning amount. Their mind especially, the subconscious mind provides various ways to spend their extra money (winning prize) to prove the correctness of their original consciousness about money i.e. their limiting belief about money.

"Wealth is the product of a man's capacity to think"
- Ayn Rand

Middle Class vs. World Class

- The Middle Class *competes* – the World Class *creates.*
- The Middle Class *avoids risk* – the World Class *manages risk.*
- The Middle Class *lives in delusion* – the World Class *lives in objective reality.*
- The Middle Class *loves to be comfortable* – the World Class *is comfortable being uncomfortable.*
- The Middle Class has a *lottery mentality* – the World Class has an *abundance mentality.*
- The Middle Class *hungers for security* – the World Class *doesn't believe that security exists.*
- The Middle Class *sacrifices growth for safety* – the World Class *sacrifices safety for growth.*
- The Middle Class *operates out of fear and scarcity* – the World Class *operates from love and abundance.*
- The Middle Class *focuses on having* – the World Class *focuses on being.*
- The Middle Class *sees themselves as victims* – the World Class *sees themselves as responsible.*
- The Middle Class *slows down* – the World Class *calms down.*
- The Middle Class is *frustrated* – the World Class is *grateful.*

- The Middle Class *has pipedreams* – the World Class *has vision.*

- The Middle Class is *ego-driven* – the World Class is *spirit-driven.*

- The Middle Class is *problem-oriented* – the World Class is *solution-oriented.*
- The Middle Class *thinks they know enough* – the World Class *is eager to learn.*

- The Middle Class *chooses fear* – the World Class *chooses growth.*

- The Middle Class is *boastful* – the World Class is *humble.*

- The Middle Class *trades time for money* – the World Class *trades ideas for money.*

- The Middle Class *denies their intuition* – the World Class *embraces their intuition.*

- The Middle Class seeks *riches* – the World Class seeks *wealth.*

- The Middle Class *believes their vision only when they see it* – the World Class *knows they will see their vision when they believe it.*

- The Middle Class *coaches through logic* – the World Class *coaches through emotion.*

- The Middle Class *speaks the language of fear* – the World Class *speaks the language of love.*

- The Middle Class *believes problem-solving stems from knowledge* – the Wold Class *believes problem-solving stems from will.*

(Content Credit to '177 Mental Toughness Secrets of the World Class' by Steve Siebold)

47. This is How You Can Raise Your Consciousness to World Class!

This is How You Can Raise Your Consciousness to World Class!

Table of Contents

To live a world class life, it is very much essential to raise your consciousness to world class. Before becoming one, you must first mentally live that life. Unless this belief sinks in your subconscious mind, it becomes very difficult to achieve this goal. Following key inputs will assist you to make your journey smooth.

School is Never Out

World class have come so far in raising their level of awareness that they realize there is always a higher level.

Average people have a worldview that says being comfortable with who and where they are in life is the key to happiness. The great ones have a worldview that says happiness is learning, growing, and becoming. School is never out for champions. The more they learn, the more they realize how much they don't know.

While average people seek mental comfort, the world class believes mental comfort is the death of growth. They live by this phrase: 'You're either growing or dying; stagnation does not exist in the universe.' Like the child who always asks "why," champions always ask questions of other top performers in an effort to get a new take on an old idea. Their ongoing mental growth reinforces their belief of another level of conscious awareness that can make them more successful, more fulfilled, and happier.

Ask yourself this critical thinking question: Am I growing or dying? If your answer is dying, make the decision today to become more aware and begin growing.

Belief is the Real Start

One of the major distinctions between average performers and champions is their belief system. Like champions, average people tend to be a product of their mental programming from childhood. People of influence, such as parents, teachers, coaches, religious leaders, and others were the primary builders and shapers of our early belief systems. In most cases, this programming is limiting because it comes from people who believe they are limited. That's why average people are saddled with a set of beliefs that are more about survival than success. Average people have been programmed to avoid pain at all costs, which promotes a 'playing not to lose' mentality.

Many world class performers were raised with these same beliefs, yet learned to reprogram themselves somewhere along the way. Champions learn how to develop empowering beliefs and invest a substantial amount of time solidifying those beliefs, mostly through their own self-talk. With guidance from coaches and mentors, champions monitor the words they use. They know reprogramming is a never-ending activity. Some people even consider this process 'positive brainwashing.' When aspiring champions learn they can program any belief they wish, and through repetitious, ongoing self-talk, build that belief into a foundation for their consciousness, it's a revelation.

A world class belief system can be created from scratch, no matter what your age, upbringing, or current lot in life. A world class belief system is a primary factor in the making of a champion, and every great performer knows it. While average people see champions as more intelligent, the champions know better. The truth is that intelligence plays a small part. Belief is the real star of the show.

The Evolution of a Belief System

Parents, teachers, coaches, ministers, friends, relatives, and other people of influence in a child's life say to the child: "This is Fact." The child accepts the elders' perception as a fact even if the elder is completely wrong. A child unconsciously ingrains these beliefs in his/her subconscious and builds habits accordingly. The child grows into an adult operating under dozens of faulty beliefs and habits but is not consciously aware of it. Adult operates under false and limiting beliefs and sets invisible boundaries for his/her life at an unconscious level.

Make a list of your most closely held beliefs, and begin the process of questioning whether they are serving you or holding you back. Question their validity. Are they relevant, or out of date? Knowing that behavior follows belief, give yourself an opportunity to discard or upgrade any beliefs that limit you.

Impact of Gratitude

The world class is famous for using non-linear thinking as a primary problem-solving strategy, and nowhere is this more apparent than when it comes to heightening their creativity. While amateurs become increasingly stressed during problem-solving, the great ones become more relaxed to enhance their creative ability. Champions know the ultimate creative force is located somewhere beyond our everyday consciousness, and they must tap this source to generate their best ideas. The secular sometimes refer to this source as the unconscious mind. The spiritual often call it God. Whatever label their belief warrants, few deny the power of the source, whatever its point of origin.

Champions know the fastest way to connect to the source is through gratitude. Thoughts and feelings of gratitude seem to elevate the performers' consciousness to a higher plane than is accessible through any other means. Professional writers call it being connected. Athletes call it being in the zone. Psychologists refer to it as a state of flow. No matter what name you assign it, the experience is the same.

It's a process that begins by letting go and mentally detaching from the end result or outcome of any task. The focus is on being, as opposed to doing. While amateurs experience this phenomenon from time to time, the great ones are able to access it much more often. They are aware of the triggers that create a mental climate conducive to this state of mind. Gratitude is the mindset of choice when they need to awaken the giant and tap their genius.

Make a list of the ten things you are most grateful for in your life, and review them every morning for the next seven days. Monitor how this activity impacts your emotions. (Excerpt is from '177 Mental Toughness Secrets of the World Class' by Steve Siebold.)

*****

48. Master Mind Principle in Accumulation of Money

Master Mind principle plays a key role in the accumulation of money. Consciously or unconsciously by using this principle, people have created history. In Master Mind, a peer-to-peer mentoring group helps members to solve their problems with input and advice from the other members.

We make plans but these plans are useless, without sufficient power to translate them into action. Power, as the term is used here, refers to the organized effort, sufficient to enable an individual to transmute desire into its monetary equivalent. An organized effort is produced through the coordination of effort of two or more people, who work toward a definite end, in a spirit of harmony.

"Power is required for the accumulation of money! Power is necessary for the retention of money after it has been accumulated!"

<u>The 'Master Mind' Principle</u>

The "Master Mind" may be defined as: "Coordination of knowledge and effort, in a spirit of harmony, between two or more people, for the attainment of a definite purpose." No individual may have great power without availing himself of the Master Mind.

Let's know the two important characteristics of the Master Mind principle, one of which is economic in nature, and the other psychic. The economic feature is obvious. Economic advantages may be created by any person who surrounds himself with the advice, counsel, and personal cooperation of a group of men who are willing to lend him wholehearted aid, in a spirit of perfect harmony. This form of cooperative alliance has been the basis of nearly every great fortune.

Your understanding of this great truth may definitely determine your financial status.

The psychic phase of the Master Mind principle is much more abstract, much more difficult to comprehend, because it has reference to the spiritual forces with which the human race, as a whole, is not well acquainted. You may catch a significant suggestion from this statement: "No two minds ever come together without, thereby, creating a third, invisible, intangible force which may be likened to a third mind."

Keep in mind the fact that there are only two known elements in the whole universe, *energy,* and *matter.* It is a well-known fact that matter may be broken down into units of molecules, atoms, and electrons. There are units of matter which may be isolated, separated, and analyzed. Likewise, there are units of energy. A human mind is a form of energy, a part of it being spiritual in nature. When the minds of two people are coordinated in a spirit of harmony, the spiritual units of energy of each mind form an affinity, which constitutes the "psychic" phase of the Master Mind.

"Wealth is no mark of God's favour. Poverty is no mark of God's displeasure." – J. C. Ryle

<u>One Plus One is More Than Two</u>

The Master Mind principle, or rather the economic feature of it, was first called to Hill's attention by Andrew Carnegie. Mr. Carnegie's Master Mind group consisted of a staff of approximately fifty men, with whom he surrounded himself, for the definite purpose of manufacturing and marketing steel. He attributed his entire fortune to the power he accumulated through this "Master Mind." Analyze the record of any man who has accumulated a great fortune and many of those who have accumulated modest fortunes, and you will find that they have either consciously, or unconsciously employed the "Master Mind" principle.

Energy is Nature's universal set of building blocks, out of which she constructs every material thing in the universe, including man, and every form of animal and vegetable life. Through a process that only Nature completely understands, she translates energy into matter. Nature's building blocks are available to man, in the energy involved in thinking! Man's brain may be compared to an electric battery. It absorbs energy from the ether, which permeates every atom of matter, and fills the entire universe.

A group of electric batteries will provide more energy than a single battery. It is also a well-known fact that an individual battery will provide energy in proportion to the number and capacity of the cells it contains. The brain functions in a similar fashion. This accounts for the fact that some brains are more efficient than others, and leads to this significant statement—a group of brains coordinated (or connected) in a spirit of harmony, will provide more thought-energy than a single brain. It's similar to just as a group of electric batteries will provide more energy than a single battery. Through this metaphor, it becomes immediately obvious that the Master Mind principle holds the secret of the power wielded by men who surround themselves with other men of brains.

Success Secret of Henry Ford

When a group of individual brains are coordinated and function in Harmony, the increased energy created through that alliance, becomes available to every individual brain in the group. It is a well-known fact that Henry Ford began his business career under the handicap of poverty, illiteracy, and ignorance. It is an equally well-known fact that, within the inconceivably short period of ten years, Mr. Ford mastered these three handicaps, and that within twenty-five years he made himself one of the richest men in America. Connect with this fact, the additional knowledge that Mr. Ford's most rapid strides became noticeable, from the time he became a personal friend of Thomas A. Edison, and you will begin to understand what the influence of one mind upon another can accomplish.

Go a step farther, and consider the fact that Mr. Ford's most outstanding achievements began from the time that he formed the acquaintances of Harvey Firestone, John Burroughs, and Luther Burbank, (each a man of great brain capacity), and you will have further evidence that power may be produced through the friendly alliance of minds. There is little if any doubt that Henry Ford is one of the best-informed men in the business and industrial world. The question of his wealth needs no discussion. Henry Ford whipped poverty, illiteracy, and ignorance by allying himself with great minds, whose vibrations of thought he absorbed into his own mind. Through his association with Edison, Burbank, Burroughs, and Firestone, Mr. Ford added to his own brainpower, the sum and substance of the intelligence, experience, knowledge, and spiritual forces of these four men. (Inspired from 'Think and Grow Rich' by Napoleon Hill)

You can use this principle for yourself as it's being used by several people and organizations across the world.

*****

49. Practice Wedge Theory to Achieve Financial Independence

Have you heard about the 'Wedge Theory' technique? It is guaranteed to make you financially independent faster than you can even imagine.

Parkinson's Law, developed by author C. Northcote Parkinson, says, ***"Expenses rise to meet income."*** This means your expenditures increase gradually in line with the gradual rise in your income. No matter how much money you make, your expenses eventually rise to consume it all, and a little bit more besides. Over time, you develop the habit of always spending whatever you earn or receive.

Brian Tracy asks his audiences this question: *"If I could wave a magic wand and double or triple your income, would that solve your financial problems?"*

Then he waits and watches their faces. Almost immediately, people raise their hands, smile, and nod. They all agree that if they could double or triple their current incomes, that would solve all their financial problems.

Then he ask a follow-up question: *"Going back to what you earned in your first job, is there anyone here who has already doubled or tripled their income?"*

After a short pause, virtually everyone in the audience raises their hands. Everyone has already doubled and tripled their incomes from their first jobs. Many have increased their incomes five and ten times from the first job they took when they left school. They still have financial problems and are in debt because they have become subject to Parkinson's Law, "Expenses rise to meet income."

"It's not how much money you make, but how much money you keep, how hard it works for you, and how many generations you keep it for." – Robert Kiyosaki

<u>Save & Invest Half of Your Future Increases</u>

Here is how the Wedge Theory works. When you ask a person to save a certain percentage of their current income, they will almost always agree that it is a good idea, but they will also claim it is not possible. To save out of your current income will mean reducing your standard of living. It may mean moving to a smaller place, driving a smaller car, eating cheaper foods, or not going out as often.

People are addicted for immediate gratification. Whenever they get the rise in their income, they are habitual to work out the ways on how to spend this additional amount. And there are plenty of ways available. Even if they can rationally agree that saving is a good idea, the actual reduction in living standards it requires is so unacceptable that they cannot discipline themselves to take the first step.

Wedge Theory is different. Instead of cutting back on your current lifestyle, you commit to save 50 percent of every increase you receive from your work from this day forward. This is something you can do because you don't yet have this money built into your daily expenditures. It is much easier for people to commit to saving money they have not yet received than it is to get people to agree to save money by cutting back on their current standard of living.

Keep on investing this saved amount, progressively by the power of compounding, you will be able to increase your income by 5 percent, 10 percent, and even 25 percent per year. To become wealthy, you must develop the habit, starting today, of saving fully 50 percent of these future increases. You can still spend the other 50 percent on whatever you like, but you must agree to save & invest half of the money you don't even have yet. This should not be hard for you.

Depending upon your age, and the rate at which your income grows, saving 50 percent of your increases in the years ahead will soon allow you to acquire an enormous amount of money. And the more money you save, the more money you will attract to yourself. By disciplining yourself and developing the habit of saving & investing half of your increases for the rest of your career, you will pay off all your debts, build an enormous financial fortress, and eventually become financially independent.

Adopt the Habits of Wealthy People

Millionaires develop a series of habits to ensure that they don't lose money and that their money grows steadily over time. You can adopt some of these habits. Like, apart from the above wedge theory, you can develop a habit of getting good financial advice before you do anything with your investment account. Your investment account, in which you keep above additional money, must be separate from your routine saving account. Ask around and find a financial advisor who has already become financially successful by investing her personal money in the areas that she recommends to you. Your ability to choose excellent financial advisors can be a critical factor in making good investment decisions to achieve financial independence.

Develop the habit of investigating before you invest in anything. The rule is, *"Spend as much time investigating the investment as you spent earning the money you are thinking of investing."*

Fast financial decisions are usually poor financial decisions. Take your time, move slowly, find out every detail of the business or investment before you ever think of writing a check. Never allow anyone to pressure you into an investment decision. Never allow yourself to feel that an investment decision is urgent and must be made immediately. If you are committed to good investment then you will get the opportunity. Even if you miss one investment opportunity, don't worry, another opportunity will appear soon. Investment opportunities are like buses; there will always be another one coming along.

Sometimes, the best investments are the ones you never make at all. Make a habit of thoroughly understanding the investment before you ever think of parting with your hard-earned money. If there is anything you do not understand or that seems too complicated for you, do not invest in that area.

Warren Buffett, one of the richest men in the world thanks to his investing acumen, refused to invest in any of the high-tech or dot-com companies during the boom of the 1990s. Everyone accused him of being out of step and old-fashioned. He simply replied, *"I don't understand these businesses and, therefore, I will not put any of my money into them."* He turned out to be right when the tech bubble burst. (Credit to 'Million Dollar Habits' by Brian Tracy).

*****

50. Implement This Painless Strategy for Financial Freedom!

Your financial freedom flow from your ability to save systematically. Most of you probably know this but you're still not doing anything about it. It means you just don't know it. Contrary to popular wisdom, knowledge is not power—it's potential power. Knowledge is not mastery. Execution is mastery. Execution will trump knowledge every day of the week.

The first step in your financial freedom journey starts with keeping aside a part of your earning. This money starts earning for you for life long. What if, you still haven't taken that first step to set aside a percentage of your earnings to save for compounded interest? Is there something holding you back? What's really going on? Could it be that you're not systematically saving money because it feels like a sacrifice—a loss—instead of a gift to yourself today and in the future?

Save More Tomorrow

Shlomo Benartzi of the UCLA Anderson School of Management has shared insightful answer to the above questions. He said, "The problem is people feel like the future is not real. So it's hard to save for the future." Benartzi and his colleague, Richard Thaler of the University of Chicago, came up with an amazing solution called Save More Tomorrow (SMarT) with a simple but powerful premise: if it hurts too much to save more money now—just wait until your next pay raise.

Save More Tomorrow is a behavioral intervention designed to make saving for retirement as easy and painless as possible. The intervention consists of a few central components. First, ask people to commit now to saving more in the future. This helps them avoid present bias. Second, planned increases in savings rates are linked to future pay raises. This minimizes the influence of loss aversion since take-home pay never decreases. Save More Tomorrow allows workers to make financial decisions closely aligned with their financial needs and long-term goals.

This "nudge" has gone on to achieve a massive scale. In 2006, it was enshrined into law as part of the Pension Protection Act of 2006 (USA), which encouraged companies to adopt the core principles of the program. Save More Tomorrow has helped several millions of people across the world to significantly boost their savings rate. (Content inspired from 'MONEY Master the Game: 7 Simple Steps to Financial Freedom' by Tony Robbins).

The Psychology Behind

How did they come up with it? First, Shlomo told Tony, they had to address the challenge of immediate gratification, or what scientists call "present bias." He gave an example: when he asked a group of students whether they wanted a banana or some chocolate for a snack, a full 75% said they wanted a banana. But two weeks later, with the choices in front of them, 80% picked the chocolate! "Self-control in the future is not a problem," said Shlomo. It's the same with saving, he told me. "We know we should be saving. We know we'll do it next year. But today we go and spend."

As a species, we're not only wired to choose today over tomorrow, but also we hate to feel like we're losing out on something. To illustrate the point, Shlomo told me about a study in which monkeys—our not-so-distant cousins—were given an apple while scientists measured their physiological responses. Enormous excitement! Then another group of monkeys was given two apples. They also displayed enormous excitement. And then one change was made: the monkeys that were given two apples had one taken away from them. They still had one apple, but what do you think happened? You guessed it. They were angry as hell! (Scientifically speaking.) Think this happens with people, too? In fact, how often does this happen with the average person? We forget what we already have, don't we?

The bottom line is, if we feel like we're losing something, we avoid it; we won't do it. That's why so many people don't save and invest. Saving sounds like you're giving something up, you're losing something today. But you're not. It's giving yourself a gift today of peace of mind, of certainty, of the large fortune in your future.

How Does It Work?

Benartzi and Thaler get around the above challenges & come up with a simple system to make saving feel painless. It aligns with our natures. As Shlomo said in a TED Talk, "Save More Tomorrow invites employees to save more maybe next year—sometime in the future when we can imagine ourselves eating bananas, volunteering more in the community, exercising more, and doing all the right things on the planet." Here's how it works: you agree to automatically save a small amount of your salary—10%, 5%, or even as little as 3%. (This is a number so small you won't even notice the difference!)

Then you commit to saving more in the future—but only when you get an increase in pay. With each pay raise, the percentage saved would automatically get a little larger, but you wouldn't feel it as a loss, because you never had it in the first place! Benartzi and Thaler first tested the Save More Tomorrow plan almost 20 years ago at a company in the Midwest where the blue-collar workers said they couldn't afford to squeeze another dime out of their paychecks. But the researchers persuaded them to let their employer automatically divert 3% of their salaries into a retirement account, and then add 3% more every time they got a pay raise. The results were amazing! After just five years and three pay raises, those employees who thought they couldn't afford to save were setting aside just under a whopping 14% of their paychecks! And 65% of them were actually saving an average of 19% of their salaries.

A Real Story for UPS Man

When you get to 19%, you're approaching the kinds of numbers that made Theodore Johnson, the UPS man, incredibly wealthy. Theodore Johnson worked for UPS and never made more than $14,000 a year and yet, in his old age, was worth more than $70 million. When he said he had no money to save, a friend told him that if he were taxed, the money would be taken out of his account and he'd never see it. So he created a tax for himself to make him wealthy. Even though he made little money, he took 20 percent of his money and it went straight into an investment account. Over more than five decades, that compounded to make him $70 million.

Start Your Financial Freedom Journey

Just go ahead and implement Save More Tomorrow in your life to enjoy financial freedom. It's painless, and it works. It's been proven time and again. Below is the chart that Shlomo uses to illustrate the impact that each increase in savings will have on an employee's lifestyle. At 3%, there's an image of a pair of sneakers—because that's all you'll be able to afford if you save only 3%! At 9%, there's a scooter. It goes all the way up to 14%, where there's a luxury car and the clear message that life is great! That's a big difference!

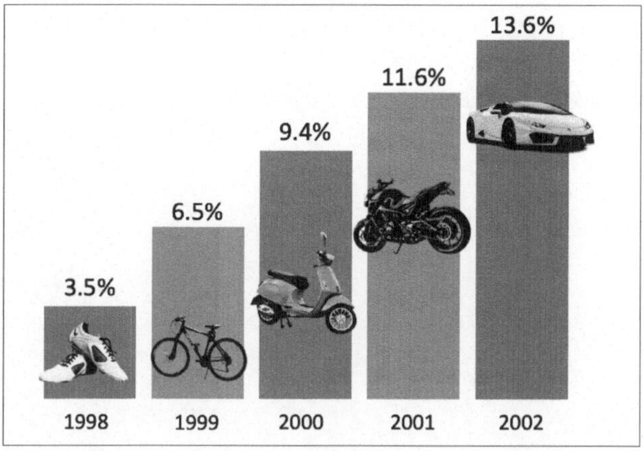

"Investing should be more like watching paint dry or watching grass grow. If you want excitement, take $800 and go to Las Vegas." – **Paul Samuelson**

*****